ABOVE THE LINE THINKING

GODLY INSIGHTS FOR TODAY

SEASON SEVEN

THOMAS A PETTERSON

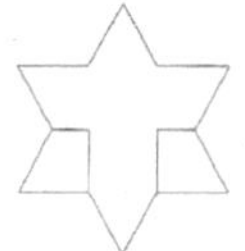

COPYRIGHT

Above The Line Thinking
Season Seven

Publishing Details:

ISBN: 978-1-7642449-3-0

Ebook Version GIFT Seasons 1-8

Season 1-7 1st Edition 2014, ePub and Mobi

Season 1-8 2nd Edition 2015, ePub and Mobi

Season 1-8 RePublished March 2023, ePub and Mobi

ISBN:9781925029895

Troubled Waters Dead Ahead Season 9:

ISBN: 979-8-231-09552-0

The Shaking & Awakening Season 8:

ISBN: 978-1-764-24490-9

Book Cover

Cover Design: bookcovers.com

Formatted with Vellum

DEDICATION

To Yahweh our Heavenly Abba;
Yeshua the author and perfecter of our faith;
Ruach HaKodesh our Counsellor and ever faithful companion and life coach without whom this book would not have been written.

Vanessa Cottam
Honouring a lifelong friendship and support.

Joy
Thank you for your extra editing and input.

With special thanks to Julie-Ann
my ever patient editor, soul mate and
love of my life!

CONTENTS

Introduction vii
Bible Quotations ix
Glossary xi
Foreword xv

1. Above The Line Thinking 1
2. The Golden Oil 10
3. Keep the Charge of the Lord 12
4. Our Great High Priest 21
5. Holy Priesthood Office 26
6. Forgiveness 29
7. Moving Forward 32
8. Disobedience 38
9. I Am The Catalyst 41
10. The Battle of the Mind 46
11. Ruach HaKodesh is Coming by Train Tomorrow 52
12. The Nursery Garden 56
13. Turn! Turn! Turn! 62
14. Has Done Is Doing Will Do 66
15. Cohanim 71
16. Tithing 75
17. The Rising 78
18. Heaven is Leaking 90

Epilogue 92

Afterword 93
About the Author 97
Also by Thomas A Petterson 99

INTRODUCTION

How do we renew our minds and free ourselves from negative thinking patterns; dwelling on past failures fuelled by shame and guilt; bound up by fears and all kinds of unbelief? Why do we always blame someone or something out of our control as the cause of all our problems? Why do we never take responsibility for our own thoughts and allow them to run rampant in our minds? Why do we allow crazy irrational, wild, destructive thoughts run around loose like uncaged animals? Why do we spend sleepless nights wrestling with our thoughts?

What is the key that will enable us all to begin thinking above the line or aligning our thinking with Yahweh's thoughts? What will give us the freedom and flexibility to follow the leading of Ruach HaKodesh each and every day and allow Him to renew our minds?

Rationalisation and self-justification is not the way out! We hold the key and it's time to humble ourselves and confess our wrong thinking as sin and repent of it! It's time to take authority over our thinking processes and with the help of Ruach HaKodesh as the Catalyst begin to take every thought captive to the obedience of Messiah. It's time to capture those crazy, lying, wild, time wasting, destructive thoughts and demolish them!

2 Corinthians 10:3-5 "For although we do live in the world, we do not wage war in a worldly way; because the weapons we use to wage war are not worldly. On the contrary, they have God's power for demolishing strongholds. We demolish arguments and every arrogance that raises itself up against the knowledge of God; we take every thought captive and make it obey the Messiah." CJB.

Romans 12:2 "Don't be conformed to this world, but be transformed by the renewing of your mind, so that you may prove what is the good, well-pleasing, and perfect will of God." WEB.

Philippians 4:8 "Finally, brothers, whatever things are true, whatever things are honorable, whatever things are just, whatever things are pure, whatever things are lovely, whatever things are of good report: if there is any virtue and if there is anything worthy of praise, think about these things." WEB.

The (key) symbol appears throughout this book to highlight key thoughts that will help you on your journey to start Thinking Above The Line.

Thomas A Petterson
Prophetic Scribe

Contact Details:
Email: giftbook@pm.me
Website: www.giftbook.net
Facebook: facebook.com/godlyinsightsfortoday

BIBLE QUOTATIONS

GLOSSARY

The following names, titles and terms are used throughout this book.

Yeshua : Jesus.

Yeshua HaMashiach : Jesus The Messiah.

Abba : Father.

Ruach HaKodesh : Holy Spirit .

Yahweh : God.

Adonai : Lord.

Tanakh : Old Testament / Old Covenant.

Brit Hadashah : New Testament / New Covenant.

Torah : First Five Books of the Hebrew Bible.

Cohen / Kohen Hagadol : High Priest.

Cohen / Kohen : Priest.

Cohanim / Kohanim : Priests.

Rosh Hashanah : Jewish New Year.

Shalom : Peace.

El Shaddai : God Almighty.

Elohim : Eternal Creator; Supreme Mighty One; The God Of Israel.

Malki-Tzedek : Melchizedek.
Gan-'Eden : Paradise
Talmidim : Disciples.
Pesach : Passover.
Ehyeh Asher Ehyeh : I am/will be what I am/will be.
Isra'el : Israel.
Tsuris : Problems - A Yiddish term.
Catalyst : An agent that provokes or speeds significant change or action.
IEDs : Improvised Explosive Devices.
Goodness : agathosune - greek word; uprightness of heart and life.
Progeny : a descendant or offspring, as in a child, plant, or animal; such descendants or offspring collectively; something that originates or results from something else; outcome; issue.
Incense : Strongs 7004 - to offer up incense; to smoke; turn into fragrance fire; as an act of worship.
Piquancy : the quality of exciting the mind pleasantly. See chapter 3 Keep The Charge Of The Lord.
Succour : to help someone, especially someone who is suffering or in need.
Omnipresent : Present everywhere simultaneously.
High Holy Days : Rosh Hashanah - Jewish New Year; Yom Kippur - Day of Atonement.
Execution Stake : Cross
Unction : the act of anointing as a rite of

consecration or healing.
Armageddon : Valley of Megiddo located in the Jezreel Valley in northern Israel. A final war between good and evil at the end of the world.
Messiah Ben Joseph : Isaiah Chapter 53
Messiah Ben David : Isaiah 9:6-7

FOREWORD

The original GIFT words are arranged in eight seasons representing various periods in my life in which a series of words were given. "Above The Line Thinking" revisits Season Seven which contains words of inspired revelation knowledge that were needed at that time but are now critical for the very uncertain days we now find ourselves in. I have found that Abba Father *(Yahweh)* always tells me what I need to know when I need to know it, but sometimes years in advance to give me time to begin to think above the line or to put it another way align my thinking with the thinking of Heaven.

I present these GIFT words that have been entrusted to me to encourage you to hear from Holy Spirit *(Ruach HaKodesh)* for yourself and it is my prayer that He will give you Godly Insights For Today (and Tomorrow) just as He did for me.

Start with a bible and a notebook. Read a passage of scripture and write down what Holy Spirit *(Ruach HaKodesh)* reveals to you. *Psalm 119:18 Open my eyes [to spiri-*

tual truth] so that I may behold Wonderful things from Your law. AMP.

The presentation of these words is in a very Hebraic style rather than Greek. So, jump in anywhere you choose. If you are a person that always reads the last chapter of a book first, these **GIFT** words will serve you well. If you are a browser, flip through them until a word, a passage or a title catches your eye.

Some of the words are challenging and often my thinking has been turned upside down. Correction and discipline are not concepts we are used to, but Abba Father disciplines and instructs those He loves *Hebrews 12:6 – "For the Lord corrects and disciplines everyone whom He loves, and He punishes, even scourges, every son whom He accepts and welcomes to His heart and cherishes." AMPC.*

Deuteronomy 8:5-6 "You shall consider in your heart that as a man disciplines his son, so Yahweh your God disciplines you. You shall keep the commandments of Yahweh your God, to walk in his ways, and to fear him". WEB.

My communication with Holy Spirit *(Ruach HaKodesh)* is by intuitive flow, sometimes word by word and sometimes in torrents. Most times I will be given a heading or a subject and sometime later I will be given the text. This can happen in a coffee shop, a library or any quiet place. It's a matter of simply going with the flow. A physical interruption does not destroy the flow and if interrupted Holy Spirit *(Ruach HaKodesh)* will pick up where we left off.

I have always known and related to the Son of God as Jesus. At age 16 I invited Him into my heart and acknowledged Jesus Christ as my Lord and Saviour. I love the name Jesus and all the songs that praise His name and all that it represents in my life. However, since first visiting Israel in 1989 and discovering the Hebrew Roots of Christianity, I now find myself more comfortable using the names Yahweh *(God)*, Yeshua *(Jesus)* and Ruach HaKodesh *(Holy Spirit)*.

This is a personal choice and I find using these names helpful in moving towards the One New Man spoken of in *Ephesians 2:14-16 For he is our peace, who made both one, and broke down the middle wall of separation, having abolished in his flesh the hostility, the law of commandments contained in ordinances, that he might create in himself one new man of the two, making peace, and might reconcile them both in one body to God through the cross, having killed the hostility through it. WEB.*

The **GIFT** words that I receive from Holy Spirit *(Ruach HaKodesh)* are in the first person. Sometimes Jesus *(Yeshua)* is speaking, sometimes it is Holy Spirit *(Ruach HaKodesh)* Himself and sometimes it is Abba Father *(Yahweh)*. It took me a while to figure out who was talking as Holy Spirit *(Ruach HaKodesh)*. relays to my spirit what He is hearing both Yeshua *(Jesus)* and Yahweh *(God)* are saying, as well as His own words. Often it is not clear until the word is complete who is speaking, but on reflection it will present itself.

You will notice that there is no tense in the words, which is only logical as Heaven, Yeshua *(Jesus)* the Messiah, Yahweh our Father in Heaven and Ruach HaKodesh the Holy Spirit dwell outside of time. Yahweh is the Great "I Am".

Exodus 3:14 God said to Moshe, "Ehyeh Asher Ehyeh [I am/will be what I am/will be]," and added, "Here is what to say to the people of Isra'el: 'Ehyeh [I Am or I Will Be] has sent me to you.'" CJB.

Exodus 3:15 God said further to Moshe, "Say this to the people of Isra'el: 'Yud-Heh-Vav-Heh [Adonai], the God of your fathers, the God of Avraham, the God of Yitz'chak and the God of Ya'akov, has sent me to you.' This is my name forever; this is how I am to be remembered generation after generation." CJB.

It is my prayer that these words of insights and instructions will be a blessing to you as they have been to me. May they assist us all in preparing our hearts and minds giving us the courage and bravery needed to face the challenges of the days we live in. May they help us to begin to see our lives and circumstances from a heavenly perspective and change our way of thinking so that it lines up with the thoughts and ways of Yahweh and His Kingdom.

Isaiah 55:8-9 "For my thoughts are not your thoughts, and your ways are not my ways," says Adonai. "As high as the sky is above the earth are my ways higher than your ways, and my thoughts than your thoughts." CJB.

May we all remain faithful to Him who has called us until He comes. Yeshua *(Jesus)* told His disciples *"I have said these things to you so that, united with me, you may have shalom. In the world, you have tsuris. But be brave! I have conquered the world!" John 16:33 CJB.*

Thomas A. Petterson
Prophet Scribe

CHAPTER 1

ABOVE THE LINE THINKING

August 9th 2008; 8th Av 5768. *Colossians 3:1-4 So if you were raised along with the Messiah, then seek the things above, where the Messiah is sitting at the right hand of God.*

Focus your minds on the things above, not on things here on earth. For you have died, and your life is hidden with the Messiah in God. When the Messiah, who is our life, appears, then you too will appear with him in glory! CJB.

Ruach HaKodesh Speaks: You are seated in heavenly places in Messiah Yeshua and the true perspective on life can only be understood from Heaven. This is especially true for understanding your own life and circumstances. From up here, you are outside the limits of time and space as you understand it and Yahweh's plan for your life is all plainly mapped out. The plans He has are not only for your welfare, but also for the blessing of others. The moment that your thinking and believing begin to align with the heavenly roadmap Heaven's resources are made available. The next step is achieved instantaneously here in Heaven. It is fact, it is reality; it has already happened; it is secure. All that needs to happen is for you to continue to walk in faith on your journey of life.

The supernatural world is of a higher order than the three-dimensional world in which you live. As fast as you can think, it happens in this world. Yahweh's power is infinite and there is no shadow of turning in Him. As He has planned for each of you, so it is and so it will be because it already is; it already has been and will be. The resources of Heaven will enable you to finish that which you have been called to do. Remember these resources have already been set aside for you ages ago. They are simply waiting for you to call them down into your situation.

James 1:16-17 Do not be deceived, my beloved brethren. Every good gift and every perfect gift is from above, and comes down from the Father of lights, with whom there is no variation or shadow of turning. NKJV.

Don't look to the left or right or try to imagine where or how Abba will meet your needs. He is new every morning; He is new every day; He is new every evening. He never has to do the same thing twice and He has an infinite variety of ways to get you your supplies right on time to get the job done. The prophetic words and scriptures are from the heavenly realm and are all above the line resources. Prophetic words are indeed the word of the Lord to you; they have currency here in Heaven and can be cashed in and will release all that is needed in abundance. The realm of the spirit operates in faith; as you set your mind on things above you will begin to understand the eternality of the Kingdom. You will begin to have more faith in the unseen than you do in the seen.

Lamentations 3:22-23 Through the Lord's mercies we are not consumed, Because His compassions fail not. They are new every morning; Great is Your faithfulness. NKJV.

Colossians 3:2 Set your mind on things above, not on things on the earth. NKJV.

Align your thinking with the thinking of Heaven and stop thinking through situations using human reasoning; it will only lead to frustration. The tree of the knowledge of good and evil tells you that on earth good and evil do coexist. The downside of this knowledge is that it can cause you to see evil at work and become fearful. The moment you do that Satan has cast a spell on you and you will begin to walk in fear. Fear is the driving force that empowers his kingdom and enslaves all who are caught up in his dragnet.

The kingdom that belongs to the tree of the knowledge of good and evil is a kingdom that can exist in your mind. It can be referred to as earthly thinking or thinking below the line. It is not wrong but will always cause you to focus on both good and evil and creates a continuing tension or a roller coaster experience. You will see and experience good and evil at war with each other in microcosms of events, communities, and peoples. Many are still under the influence of the rulers of darkness, principalities, wickedness in high places, and territorial demons. They are contending against good, particularly good deeds and the righteous actions of My people. If you are to get off the roller coaster you must begin to think above the line.

Ask such questions as: *"What is Abba trying to change in me?"* or *"What am I learning through this contention and strife?" "Is there something that is not right in me?"* or *"Do I need to keep standing in faith?"*

All the time be careful not to contend with flesh, particularly your brothers and sisters in Messiah. As you begin to lift your focus to the heavenly places the answers you seek will be revealed and released. They have always been there but sometimes, you become blind to the supernatural eternal truths because you are engaged in a spiritual battle.

Romans 8:5 For those who identify with their old nature set their minds on the things of the old nature, but those who identify with the Spirit set their minds on the things of the Spirit. CJB.

The answers are up here. You can't cause a person to stop believing what they do or acting and behaving the way that they do. As you forgive them and look to Heaven, the reason will become clear and you will either be corrected and disciplined or encouraged and emboldened. The experience either way will prepare you for the next step in your destiny.

🗝 The Kingdom that belongs to the Tree of Life holds the knowledge of Yahweh. It encompasses the knowledge of all things as they truly are in Heaven. Anything from the tree of knowledge of good and evil that attempts to exalt itself above the knowledge of Yahweh will be vaporised. The moment that it raises its head above the line or tries to make entry into the supernatural Kingdom of Heaven it ceases to exist. Lies or contentions with the perfect will of Yahweh will never make entrance. They cannot breach even the remotest part of the Kingdom. It just won't happen.

🗝 The kingdom that belongs to the knowledge of good and evil has the knowledge of the flesh and will cause you to think below the line. When you try to do something about the evil in your own strength, no matter how well-intentioned, you will end up in the courtroom of Heaven where Satan accuses the brethren night and day.

Revelation 12:10 Then I heard a loud voice saying in heaven, "Now salvation, and strength, and the kingdom of our God, and the power of His Christ have come, for the accuser of our brethren, who accused them before our God day and night, has been cast down." NKJV.

Yahweh Speaks: Stop contending with people and events in the light of past experiences. Don't focus solely on how I have acted up till now. Stop thinking only from a human perspective and begin to think above the line. If people are giving you a hard time, be assured that I'm teaching you something. I am using the situations to prepare you for your destiny. Don't fight it. Give it to Me. Learn your lesson and learn it well by asking Me what it is that I'm teaching you. Nothing happens by chance or by random occurrence.

I have planned these things to shape you like a potter shapes vessels of clay. I will also shape you as a gardener prunes and tends the shrubs in his garden. At the appointed time, you will shine. You will be a reflection of My nature in the world. This includes your family, friends, and all I tell you to share with. You will jointly fit together with other works of My hands to complete My masterpiece. This masterpiece is the beautiful radiant bride of My beloved Son.

Isaiah 64:8 But now, O Lord, You are our Father; We are the clay, and You our potter; And all we are the work of Your hand. NKJV.

Look up, think up, act up, believe up, worship up, praise up above the line of your current thinking. When you pray, see yourself before the golden altar in the heavenly throne room. Look for the angels of Heaven; look into the eyes of My beautiful Son. Enjoy the colours, lights and fragrances of Heaven. I made them for you to enjoy. Be more heavenly minded than you ever have been before. Stir up Ruach HaKodesh within you and ask Him to teach you obedience. This way you can enter into the fullness of My joy.

Take all of My Words to you; savour them, eat them, live them, and do them. They are your bread that I have made available for you. Come dine with Me in My Heaven, drink daily of the new wine that is prepared for you. You are a citizen of the Kingdom of Heaven, with full throne room rights. You have full and open access to the Kingdom. Do not let your fears and unbelief stop you from thinking and living above the line. Others have shared their experiences with you and you have seen firsthand the power that is available. It is accessible to all who will press in and lay hold of the promises in My Word. Dwelling in heavenly places has never been easier because I have opened many more portals and doorways into the heavenlies.

Come eat of the Tree of Life and your eyes will be opened to My way of thinking and My way of doing things here in Heaven. You will not understand My wisdom but you can certainly appreciate it and be its beneficiary. I want you to know Me. All that I have done in the world is so that man can know Me and fellowship intimately with Me. My Spirit will guide you into all truth and everything that you need to know to lead a full and satisfying life. I am your Abba. I love you not only with a human father's love; I love you with a love that passes understanding in its depth, width and intensity.

Revelation 2:7 Those who have ears, let them hear what the Spirit is saying to the Messianic communities. To him winning the victory I will give the right to eat from the Tree of Life which is in God's Gan-'Eden. CJB.

John 16:13 However, when He, the Spirit of truth, has come, He will guide you into all truth; for He will not speak on His own authority, but whatever He hears He will speak; and He will tell you things to come. NKJV.

I drew you to Myself lovingly and deliberately because I couldn't bear to be away from you. I want you to love Me in the same way. You are My progeny; the seed that you were formed from was a part of Myself. You are My offspring and you have My nature and attributes deep within you. You will discover all that you are in Me and we will have deep and meaningful communications. However, you must begin thinking the thoughts of Heaven. Your thoughts must be centred on Myself and the Kingdom.

Isaiah 55:8-9 "For my thoughts are not your thoughts, and your ways are not my ways," says Adonai. "As high as the sky is above the earth are my ways higher than your ways, and my thoughts than your thoughts". CJB.

Nothing is impossible for you if you will only believe. Eat of the Tree of Life, enjoy and experience Messiah in you, the hope of glory. *Colossians 1:27 To them God willed to make known what are the riches of the glory of this mystery among the Gentiles: which is Christ in you, the hope of glory. NKJV.*

Daily partake of this Tree and ask Me to open up your spiritual senses to experience all that I am. My knowledge is established forever. My Word is settled forever in Heaven. It is above all power and dominions and principalities and rulers and wickedness in high places. Pull down the stronghold of unbelief in your mind. Speak to the mountain of unbelief that you have built over a lifetime and command it to be cast into the sea. This will allow you to see and behold Me and the Kingdom more clearly. *Mark 11:23 Yes! I tell you that whoever does not doubt in his heart but trusts that what he says will happen can say to this mountain, 'Go and throw yourself into the sea!' and it will be done for him. CJB.*

The mountain that has been built in your mind, through past experiences, is a fruit of the tree of the knowledge of good and evil. It is not a dependable mountain and rather than helping you to get closer to Me it has become a religious mountain. This mountain blocks your view of Heaven and it must be cast down. Remember that I am new every morning, and I rarely do things the same way twice. All that this mountain symbolises is your current understanding of who I am. If you are ever going to think above the line you need to cast this mountain into the sea.

New and fresh each moment is who I am. You don't need to climb a mountain of past experiences to get close to Me. It has now become a hindrance to the new and fresh truths that I would reveal to you. There are plenty of beautiful mountains here in the Kingdom for you to climb and explore; they are true and faithful representations of real experiences in Me yet to be had. My mountains are glorious, full of glory and beauty and splendour beyond comprehension. Get rid of your mountain and let Me show you some of My beautiful handiwork. They will satisfy your every longing; not only here and now in this lifetime but for all of eternity.

Thinking has power in Heaven and My eternal truths are often transmitted by thought. Spiritual supernatural thinking is a valid form of communication in the Kingdom and here on earth. Often I prompt My servants by My Spirit to be thinking My thoughts and communicate them at the appropriate time. The streams of thoughts come from the stream that is continually flowing throughout the earth. (*See The Battle of the Mind chapter 10*).

It is My communication network here on earth. Through it, I long to convey heavenly truths. I long to give instruction and offer wisdom to all who have tuned their ears to hear and their eyes to see.

James 1:5 Now if any of you lacks wisdom, let him ask God, who gives to all generously and without reproach; and it will be given to him. CJB.

It is indeed My Glory-Net which comes with video, audio and fragrances. It is an experiential communication network that puts the internet to shame by comparison. When My thoughts become your thoughts and you release them into the atmosphere My power is released. Daily connect to My Glory-Net to see and hear and learn what to do in every day life.

Do as My Son did. Speak what you see and hear into the situations in your life. Don't trust your own thoughts.

Proverbs 3:5-7 Trust in the Lord with all your heart, And lean not on your own understanding; In all your ways acknowledge Him, And He shall direct your paths. Do not be wise in your own eyes; Fear the Lord and depart from evil. NKJV.

- Mimic My Son Yeshua!
- Be directed by Ruach HaKodesh each and every day!
- Think the thoughts of Heaven!
- Live as Yeshua lived!
- Do as He did!
- Seek to find My perfect will for your life!
- It really is that simple and powerful!

It's time to Think Above The Line!

CHAPTER 2

THE GOLDEN OIL

December 17th 2008; 20th Kislev 5769.

Vision: *I saw Yeshua coming towards me saturated and dripping with Golden Oil. He stretched out His arms towards me, dripping with oil, inviting me to come to Him and be embraced by Him.*

Questions: *Why is Yeshua covered with Oil? Why does He want me to embrace Him and get covered with this Oil too?*

Ruach HaKodesh Speaks: Yeshua is The Anointed One and He is indeed anointed with the Golden Oil of Heaven and literally drips the Golden Oil wherever He goes. This Anointing Oil has its source and origin from the Tree of Life that grows in Heaven's garden. The Golden Oil was produced by Yahweh Himself who anointed His precious Son from head to toe with this peculiar Oil as the unction to fulfil the office of the King of Kings; being officially recognised on His return from the defeat of Satan. The Oil comes from the Tree of Life because it symbolises the eternal life that was won for all mankind and is a foundation stone of the Kingdom itself.

At times Yeshua appears with his entire being saturated

in this Oil dripping from head to toe; because He is clothed in Yahweh's Glory and dripping with His nature. Yahweh Himself lavishly anointed Him because He is worthy to receive all honour and praise; the Golden Oil is a public setting apart and endorsement of who He is; King of Kings, Lord of Lords, Abba's Holy Anointed one; dripping with the very nature of Yahweh Himself; the Golden Oil representing His abiding cohesive thick righteous covering of Glory. It covers and clings and abides upon Yeshua in an ever-increasing supply; a true overflow of Yahweh's nature; expressing the never-ending nature of the works of Yahweh.

Yeshua comes to you with outstretched arms because He wishes to embrace you and all who come to Him, so that you too will be covered with this Golden Anointing Oil and share with Him the delights of the true nature of Yahweh. This Oil will cover you as a thick heavy garment; it will saturate you not only on the outside; the Oil will work its way through to your inner most being; changing, transforming, renewing, reshaping you into the image of the Son and a reflection of the nature of our Abba in Heaven.

The Golden Oil never runs out and will always flow from Yeshua Himself to you. As you embrace Him and as you cover yourself with this Oil it will begin to transform you and a measure of His divine Kingly Anointing will come upon you. Unlike Yeshua your supply will run out because He is your author and source of the Golden Oil. As you draw near to Him the Golden Oil will cover you; and His Kingly Anointing's divine nature will work in your life and ministry.

Zechariah 4:12 I asked him the second time, "What are these two olive branches, which are beside the two golden spouts that pour the ***golden oil*** *out of themselves?" WEB.*

CHAPTER 3

KEEP THE CHARGE OF THE LORD

October 8th 2005; 5th Tishrei 5766.

2 Chronicles 13:10-11 "But as for us, Yahweh is our God, and we have not forsaken him. We have priests serving Yahweh, the sons of Aaron, and the Levites in their work. They burn to Yahweh every morning and every evening burnt offerings and sweet incense. They also set the show bread in order on the pure table, and care for the gold lamp stand with its lamps, to burn every evening; for we keep the instruction of Yahweh our God, but you have forsaken him." WEB.

Salt Covenant 2 *Chronicles 13:4-5 Then Abijah stood on Mount Zemaraim, which is in the hill country of Ephraim, and said, "Listen to me, Jeroboam and all Israel: Do you not know that the Lord God of Israel gave the rule over Israel forever to David and his sons by a covenant of salt? NASB.*

Abba Speaks: I am the eternal one and the salt covenant is My seal of approval forever over the affairs of all I have encompassed into My great eternal plans. My covenant is eternal; when I deal with, accept, approve or commission a person, a people, a tribe, a nation, I indeed enter into a salt covenant as that is My nature. A covenant that I make with you is eternal by nature because I am eternal. Just as the blood covenant is eternal by nature so are all My dealings with mankind; there is always an eternal aspect that many have not even regarded or thought about.

The covenant of salt I made with David long outlived him. It continued all the way to the arrival of the prophesied Eternal One, My Son Yeshua; the eternal heir ruling not only as King of the Jews; but indeed as the King of Kings and Lord of Lords. He is forever enthroned in Heaven and ruling over all the Kingdom and realms of Glory forever. You are the salt of the earth but that which is begun in your life will have an eternal expression here in Heaven.

All the offerings were offered up with salt to symbolically represent the eternal nature of Myself present in each offering and My eternal commitment to the Tanakh. The Brit Hadashah is also salted with My presence that affirms I have made an eternal commitment to those that have received My Son Yeshua by faith into their lives.

I am present at the new birth and in type I have made a salt covenant with you that is your guarantee that the covenant made with you is an eternal one; beginning here in this lifetime but extending all the way into eternity. To enter into an eternal covenant with Me you will need to become eternal also.

1 Corinthians 15:50 and 53 Now I say this, brethren, that flesh and blood cannot inherit the kingdom of God; nor does the perishable inherit the imperishable.

For this perishable must put on the imperishable, and this mortal must put on immortality. NASB-1995.

You are the salt of the earth because My eternal nature will manifest itself through you. You are My people and you will be full of hope and dreams and promises; men and women given to inspirational ideas; concepts that bring life and joy and peace to all of mankind. There should be genius and great wealth and prosperity for all who are called by My Name because you are My salty ones that add zest to life.

Come look again at My promises and My Word; look again but with a more eternal view. My Word does not end when your life ends. My promises to you are eternal. My Word is eternal. My relationship with you is eternal. Ask Ruach HaKodesh to open your eyes so that you may see what you have not seen before; that you are in a Salt Covenant with Almighty Yahweh Himself - El Shaddai and I am well able to fulfil My Word in your life. But there is so much more that My Word promises; it is another dimension in thinking. Begin to explore My eternal nature. I am Yahweh Elohim, the eternal creator.

Genesis 1:1 In the beginning, God (a) created the heavens and the earth. Footnotes (a) The Hebrew word rendered "God" is "אֱלֹהִים" (Elohim). WEB.

It does not simply mean that I am eternal and create universes, worlds, people, animals, trees, the oceans and all that you have understood by creation; but rather think of Me as one who is creating eternal things after My own image and nature.

Earth and the world that you know is transitory, but eternal in the sense that it will long outlast mankind and all that it was intended and created to be; but you and every precious one who is born again is an eternal creation of My hands that has a beginning but no end. Whatever is achieved by you and through you is an expression of who you are. It is a revealing of your true eternal nature but whatever you achieve; even to the saving of the whole world; is only the beginning of who you are and who I created you to be. It can only find its completeness and total fulfilment here in Heaven and the greater realms of Glory.

Under the Old Covenant the priesthood faithfully performed their duties; *2 Chronicles 13:10-11 But as for us, the Lord is our God, and we have not forsaken Him. We have priests ministering to the Lord who are sons of Aaron, and Levites for their service.*

They offer to the Lord every morning and every evening burnt sacrifices and incense of sweet spices; they set in order the showbread on the table of pure gold and attend to the golden lampstand, that its lamps may be lighted every evening. For we keep the charge of the Lord our God, but you have forsaken Him. AMPC.

You also must Keep the Charge of the Lord your God. In type the priests met with Myself represented by the ministry at the golden altar; My Son represented by the ministry at the table of showbread; Ruach HaKodesh represented by the ministry at the lamp stand. We are all present in type in the acts of service rendered by Aaron and the Levites. Salt is present in the incense that is offered on the golden altar and the sweet aroma that arose had intrinsically embedded in it the promise of the eternal covenant of grace yet to come. Under the New Covenant you are able to come as holy priests to Me and offer up day and night sacrifices of praise and worship at the golden altar because the sin offering has been taken care of forever; giving you free and open access as never before.

Romans 12:1 I exhort you, therefore, brothers, in view of God's mercies, to offer yourselves as a sacrifice, living and set apart for God. This will please him; it is the logical "Temple worship" for you. CJB.

1 Peter 2:4-5 As you come to him, the living stone, rejected by people but chosen by God and precious to him, you yourselves, as living stones, are being built into a spiritual house to be cohanim set apart for God to offer spiritual sacrifices acceptable to him through Yeshua the Messiah. CJB.

My Son Yeshua is the bread of Heaven and is always present and you are to eat of His flesh and drink of His blood which are eternal by nature. The misunderstanding of the prophetic meaning of these words caused many to draw back because they thought only of the here and now; the thought of eating flesh and drinking blood so repugnant and heathen that they turned away from following My Son. The understanding can only come as you view the eternal nature of the blood covenant; that it is eternal and extends from its beginnings here on earth to be the assurance and guarantee of the eternal covenant.

You will need to be changed to enter Heaven and as you receive by faith the eternal flesh and eternal blood; you are able to make the transition from flesh to spirit. It is a symbolic receiving of the eternal nature of Myself and My Son so that your flesh shall become like His flesh and your blood like His blood.

1 Corinthians 15:53-54 For this perishable must put on the imperishable, and this mortal must put on immortality. But when this perishable will have put on the imperishable, and this mortal will have put on immortality, then will come about the saying that is written, DEATH IS SWALLOWED UP in victory. NASB.

It is as though Yeshua Himself now lives in you, it is His spiritual body within, it is His spiritual blood within you; *"it is no longer I who live, but the Messiah lives in me."*

Galatians 2:20 I have been crucified with Christ [in Him I have shared His crucifixion]; it is no longer I who live, but Christ (the Messiah) lives in me; and the life I now live in the body I live by faith in (by adherence to and reliance on and complete trust in) the Son of God, Who loved me and gave Himself up for me. AMP.

By symbolically eating His flesh and drinking His blood you are becoming like Him; you are receiving His eternal nature into your spirit man; you are feeding on Him; there is an impartation; a spirit to spirit blood transfusion; an enabling; a divine encounter; miraculous new birth; healing for sick bodies; long life; skills; gifts and abilities. These resources are found in the nature of My Son and the scripture was meant to show that you cannot receive anything into yourself unless you eat of it and drink of it. Just as you consume food and drink water, so too are you to consume the eternal nature of My Son.

If you eat something or drink something it becomes a part of you. There is no better example of making something a part of yourself. It's good enough to eat! Eat and drink of Him until you are satisfied; for He is life, health and meat to your spirit man. My Ruach HaKodesh is always present with you and is the working interface that you have with Heaven itself. He will lead you into how to Keep the Charge of the Lord.

I have with you as I did with David a covenant of salt; an eternal covenant. Your part in this as My covenant partner is to Keep the Charge of the Lord while ever you are here on earth. The greater eternal aspect of this charge will be revealed in Heaven; you are learning that all the symbols and types that are recorded in My Word have their origins from the Kingdom of Heaven; the moment that you see them you will understand how they have always pointed to the way everlasting; the types and patterns having their fulfilment and expression here in My glorious Heaven.

Incense : Strong's 7004 - offer up incense; to smoke; turn into fragrance by fire; as an act of worship.

Exodus 30:7-9 Aaron shall burn fragrant incense on it; he shall burn it every morning when he trims the lamps.

And when Aaron sets up the lamps at twilight, he shall burn incense. There shall be perpetual incense before the Lord throughout your generations.

You shall not offer any strange incense on this altar, or burnt offering or meal offering; and you shall not pour out a drink offering on it. NASB.

Revelation 8:3-4 Another angel came and stood at the altar, holding a golden censer; and much incense was given to him, so that he might add it to the prayers of all the saints on the golden altar which was before the throne.

And the smoke of the incense, with the prayers of the saints, went up before God out of the angel's hand. NASB-1995.

1 Timothy 2:8 I desire therefore that in every place men should pray, without anger or quarrelling or resentment or doubt [in their minds], lifting up holy hands. AMPC.

Revelation 5:8 When He had taken the scroll, the four living creatures and the twenty-four elders fell down before the Lamb, each one holding a harp and golden bowls full of incense, which are the prayers of the saints. NASB.

Covenant of Salt:

Season Your Speech; *Colossians 4:6 Let your speech always be with grace, seasoned with salt, that you may know how you ought to answer each one. NKJV.*

Salt of the Earth; *Matthew 5:13 "You are salt for the Land. But if salt becomes tasteless, how can it be made salty again? It is no longer good for anything except being thrown out for people to trample on." CJB.*

Salt With Fire; *Mark 9:49 "For everyone will be salted with fire." NASB.*

Salt Can Lose its Savour; *Luke 14:34-35 Salt is excellent. But if even the salt becomes tasteless, what can be used to season* *it? It is fit for neither soil nor manure — people throw it out. Those who have ears that can hear, let them hear! CJB.*

Ruach HaKodesh Speaks: Yahweh never loses his savour. He is the salty one. You are salty because He is salty. He called you the salt of the earth because you are to bring flavour, enrichment, enhancement, enjoyment to life because you have the light of life within you. You can only maintain your saltiness by contact with the salty one. As you savour His flavour, He flavours your savour. He is the only antidote.

Without continual contact with Him you will become tasteless; unable to be the salt of the earth or even fit for any good thing.

Salt is defined as - "anything that gives liveliness, freshness, piquancy or pungency to anything".

Leviticus 2:13 Every grain offering of yours, moreover, you shall season with salt, so that the salt of the covenant of your God shall not be lacking from your grain offering; with all your offerings you shall offer salt. NASB-1995.

Numbers 18:19 All the offerings of the holy gifts, which the sons of Israel offer to the LORD, I have given to you and your sons and your daughters with you, as a perpetual allotment. It is an everlasting covenant of salt before the LORD to you and your descendants with you. NASB-1995.

2 Chronicles 13:5 Do you not know that the LORD GOD of Israel gave the rule over Israel forever to David and his sons by a covenant of salt? NASB.

Ezekiel 43:24 You shall present them before the LORD, and the priests shall throw salt on them, and they shall offer them up as a burnt offering to the LORD. NASB-1995.

Abba Speaks: The Time is Now! For the time has now come for you to be about My business. You will need to relay the foundations; as I need much more time to instruct you in all matters. I am at work in all that you are doing and I'm bringing all things together for now is the appointed time.

Rise up from your grief and disappointments and let them go for I am Elohim in all that has happened in your life. Now it is time to speak life into your situation and I will release My resurrection power into your body and your spirit to enable you to rise up above the circumstances, attitudes and tactics of the evil one that have had you bound. I have equipped you at deep levels and prepared you for all that is to come. Let Me be your only guide from now on; concentrate on your relationship with Me.

Enjoy Me; let go of all your worries and anxieties for I have gone before you and will release all the resources you will need to fulfil My will for your life. Do not despair any longer of what the enemy has done to you; he thinks he has succeeded but now it is time to come forth as it were from the grave and set your face only to do My will.

Keep The Charge Of The Lord!

CHAPTER 4

OUR GREAT HIGH PRIEST

Rosh Hashana Jewish New Year. October 4th 2005; 1st Tishrei 5766.

Hebrews 3:1 Therefore, brothers whom God has set apart, who share in the call from heaven, think carefully about Yeshua, whom we acknowledge publicly as God's emissary and as cohen gadol. CJB.

In the context of Keeping the Charge of the Lord, Yeshua is the great high priest; we are called to the priesthood to minister with Him to Abba and on behalf of others in the world.

Hebrews 5:5-6 So neither did the Messiah glorify himself to become cohen gadol; rather, it was the One who said to him, "You are my Son; today I have become your Father."

Also, as he says in another place, "You are a cohen forever, to be compared with Malki-Tzedek." CJB.

Yeshua is not before Abba to pray for our fallen selves to be saved and brought under His blood. His function is not to remain as the slain Lamb so that we can be reconciled to Yahweh. By His death He atoned for our sins and redeemed us once and for all and we must appropriate cleansing, forgiveness, remission of sins by standing in faith upon the promises of Yahweh and the covenant cut in Yeshua's blood.

Yeshua is before Abba not to plead for forgiveness for our sins because that is always freely available at all times simply by praying and believing. He is the high priest of our confession; He leads us in praising and worshipping Abba. He helps us to come into a deeper, fuller and more meaningful relationship with Yahweh. He teaches us to seek Abba's will and lay aside our selfish ambitions. He is not there to help us get what we want, but rather to help us see Yahweh our Abba through His eyes; to teach us the hidden mysteries of who Yahweh is and to help us daily lay down all dependence upon ourselves and our own abilities.

He is calling us to come up higher and commune with Abba; to see into Abba's heart and look at the world through His eyes; to give us the wisdom to know what to do in each situation, to reveal to us any error in our thinking; to help us keep religion out of our relationship with Himself and with Abba. He teaches us to be holy priests by example; He will take us into the courts of Heaven to behold the wisdom, glory and holiness of Yahweh. Each trip to the throne room changes us because we are beholding His Glory. We are obtaining grace and mercy from the throne of Yahweh not only for ourselves; but for all and everyone that we bring before the throne.

As holy priests we are bringing others before the throne not just ourselves; and in performing our duty we are blessed and touched and healed because being in His presence will do that without you ever having to ask; it goes with the office. It is our responsibility to bring all those that are under our charge or authority before Yahweh so that we can obtain mercy and grace for them just as Yeshua has done for us. There is joy, there is singing, there is dancing there is music there is fragrance in the throne room; there is life, there is light, there is energy, there is love indescribable, beyond imagination, beyond words. Coming into the throne room is an experience of the Spirit.

As with all encounters with the eternal each time is different and unique; but we will always walk away changed by His glorious presence forever. Yeshua offered one sacrifice for sins forever and sat down at the right hand of Abba waiting until his enemies will be made into a foot stool for His feet.

Hebrews 10:12-14 Whereas this One [Christ], after He had offered a single sacrifice for our sins [that shall avail] for all time, sat down at the right hand of God, Then to wait until His enemies should be made a stool beneath His feet.

For by a single offering He has forever completely cleansed and perfected those who are consecrated and made holy. AMPC.

Abba Speaks: The fire of the burnt offering spoke of a cleansing act; a finish to the death process; a prevention of all the rotting and stench resulting from death and signified the completion of the sacrifice. This aroma was acceptable to Me because it spoke of the end of the sin or lawless deed. The sacrifice had been made, atonement achieved and I was satisfied that it was finished.

When My Son Yeshua spoke from the execution stake the words "it is finished" He signified that the sin sacrifice for all of mankind had been completed - the Battle for your Souls had been won! Three days later His earthly body was resurrected and over 500 people witnessed and testified that death itself had been defeated and the fear of death had lost its sting.

1 Corinthians 15:6 and afterwards he was seen by more than five hundred brothers at one time, the majority of whom are still alive, though some have died. CJB.

Psalm 16:8-11 I have set Yahweh always before me. Because he is at my right hand, I shall not be moved. Therefore my heart is glad, and my tongue rejoices. My body shall also dwell in safety.

For you will not leave my soul in Sheol, neither will you allow your holy one to see corruption. You will show me the path of life. In your presence is fullness of joy. In your right hand there are pleasures forever more. WEB.

My Glory was released in great measure that day to establish the Kingdom of My Son and crown Him as the King of Kings and Lord of Lords. As the great high priest He laid down His own body and life as a living sacrifice. He who was without sin and who had fulfilled all the requirements of the old covenant became the Lamb of Yahweh that takes away the sin of the world; past, present and future. As He laid down that which is a human's most prized possession, the ultimate sacrifice of His own life; He set in place an example for you that you are to follow.

Paul wrote in the epistle to the Romans this important principle for all who are to be holy priests unto the Lord. *Romans 12:1-2 Therefore I urge you, brethren, by the mercies of God, to present your bodies a living and holy sacrifice, acceptable to God, which is your spiritual service of worship.*

And do not be conformed to this world, but be transformed by the renewing of your mind, so that you may prove what the will of God is, that which is good and acceptable and perfect. NASB-1995.

As holy priests there is no sacrificing for the sins of others; just the sacrifice of yourselves and sacrifices of praise to be offered up continually day and night; in grateful thankfulness for all that I have done for you, what I am doing and what I will do for you and all that are under your authority.

Hebrews 10:19 So, brothers, we have confidence to use the way into the Holiest Place opened by the blood of Yeshua. CJB.

Hebrews 8:1-2 Now in the things which we are saying, the main point is this; we have such a high priest, who sat down on the right hand of the throne of the Majesty in the heavens, a servant of the sanctuary and of the true tabernacle, which the Lord pitched, not man. WEB.

Hebrews 9:2 For there was a tabernacle prepared. In the first part were the lamp stand, the table, and the show bread; which is called the Holy Place. WEB.

Hebrews 13:15 Through Him then, let us continually offer up a sacrifice of praise to God, that is, the fruit of lips that give thanks to His name. NASB-1995.

Yeshua the Messiah is Our Great High Priest!

CHAPTER 5

HOLY PRIESTHOOD OFFICE

July 16th 2006; 20th Tamuz 5766.

Yahweh our heavenly Abba wants us to be like Himself. We were created in His image to be a praise of His Glory and to represent Him in the world.

Ephesians 1:12 to the end that we should be to the praise of his glory, we who had before hoped in Christ. WEB.

We are born in sin and our nature is contrary to everything that Yahweh our heavenly Abba is. We are born again into the world of the spirit; life for us begins anew as we begin to take on the likeness of Yahweh and grow up into Him. We are physically born of flesh and this temple becomes the residence of the new spiritual you when you are born again.

It is only as we tune in our spirits to Heaven itself that we can begin to become like Yeshua and like Abba. Dying to self and earthly ambitions; desiring with all of our hearts to be like Him; is the first step on the journey to becoming like Him. Learning to forgive others for their transgressions against you is the beginning of love; being able to look past what a person is doing or saying and being able to love them despite what they say and do; is the beginning of maturity in the life of the Spirit.

People that are bound by strong demonic influences can act out many unseemly things until they are set free. The ability to forgive is foremost in the life of the holy priesthood; it is foundational if we are to have the heart of Abba and understand His love. If He responded to us the way we do to others in the body of Messiah there would be no body of Messiah; with good justification He could have wiped us all out.

Looking always to a person's potential in Messiah is a focus that we must develop in our dealings with our brothers and sisters in Messiah. Whether we agree or disagree with a person's theology is not where our focus should be; but rather on what Yahweh is revealing to us about what others can and will be if they go the distance and obey the leading and promptings of Ruach HaKodesh.

The holy priesthood is always looking to the future as if it is fact; speaking words of life, prophecy and encouragement into the hearts and spirits of all who are brought to them for counsel or prayer. The holy priesthood are men and women who are dedicated to the plans of Yahweh being established in the world; who have seen the future direction that Yahweh our Abba wishes to take in the lives of individuals and the body of Messiah as a whole. They are more focused on what people are becoming than who they are and who they have been.

This picture or understanding of Yahweh's plans and purposes is gained by spending much time in the presence of Yahweh; hearing, loving and obeying Him and observing the comings and goings in the Kingdom of Heaven. They will instinctively know the direction or plans that Abba has for each person and group of people; it will fit into their understanding of the realms of Glory and how it is being released throughout the earth.

Prayer and prophecy are the mainstays of the holy priesthood; ever longing to be close to Abba in Heaven and getting as close as they can to the throne room and Abba Himself. The Glory of Yahweh will rise upon the holy priesthood. He stamps His authority on those that are to lead the body of Messiah into maturity in these last days. Pretenders and all who are covered with their own glory will not be able to stand in the presence of Yahweh's authority and His true servants; the beguiling spirits within them will lose their power and ability to seduce the body of Messiah. They will be unable to beguile and seduce men and women and strip them bare as they have been doing.

Ruach HaKodesh Speaks: It is time to pray, to draw near, and to humble yourself so that I can equip you to be My true holy priesthood in these last days. Come My servant, My love, My joy, enter into the presence of your Lord this day and do not let go until I have trained and equipped you to be a part of My holy priesthood to your generation.

CHAPTER 6

FORGIVENESS

September 2nd 2025; 9th Elul 5785.

Ruach HaKodesh Speaks: Forgiveness is foundational for spiritual fitness. Unforgiveness is of the flesh; forgiveness is of the spirit. How long does it take to drop something? That's how long it should take you to forgive others. Learn to keep short accounts on others' failings and shortcomings. Forgive as you have been forgiven. Practice forgiving ahead of time. In your morning prayers forgive those who will offend you in the course of the day. If you live each day with a forgiving attitude, you will be able to forgive more readily and stay focused on the work at hand. This will keep you fit for the Master's Work.

Colossians 3:13 Be gentle and forbearing with one another and, if one has a difference (a grievance or complaint) against another, readily pardoning each other; even as the Lord has [freely] forgiven you, so must you also [forgive]. AMPC.

Yeshua Speaks: Unforgiveness blinds you to the greater battle that is against you; whilst you are recovering from hurts suffered because of your inability to forgive, the enemy is setting in place tactics to destroy you and My plans for your life. That is why I instruct you again and again to let it drop, forgive, forget and focus on Me. You are vulnerable and exposed while ever you hold hurts and offences in your heart. Your heart cannot be full of My love if you cannot look past offences and wrongs done to you.

When you are offended you are in danger of being joined together with the evil one against your brother or sister in Messiah. Unforgiveness can hold you bound and stop you moving on to My plans and purposes for your life. Learn to have a forgiving attitude. Forgive ahead of time and surround yourself with a wall of forgiveness. Learn to quickly forgive others and their offences against you from your heart. Let them all go! Drop them and move on!

You must always be full of My love which you will learn by observation, illustration and practice. My love is forgiving, it does not overlook sins or embrace sin; it is forgiving because this divine act releases more of My love and frees you up to be sensitive to what My Spirit is saying to you in any given instance. Practice forgiveness; walk in forgiveness; and forgive ahead of time as I have shown you. Make it a habit of your life.

I will give you the boldness to address issues in your own life and others' lives with My pure love. My pure love is only able to be released in an atmosphere of forgiveness and wisdom and understanding. My goodness and forgiving nature must be a fact in your walk with Me; a firm foundation of your Messiah-like character. This must be set in place so that you can always be free to hear My voice and not have the lines of communication to Heaven severed by offences, hurts and unforgiveness.

Have a Forgiving Attitude: *Mark 11:25-26 And whenever you stand praying, if you have anything against anyone, forgive him and let it drop (leave it, let it go), in order that your Father*

Who is in heaven may also forgive you your [own] failings and shortcomings and let them drop.

But if you do not forgive, neither will your Father in heaven forgive your failings and shortcomings. AMPC.

Unforgiveness leads to bitterness, anger, divisions, enmity and strife, and these are all practices of the flesh.

Ephesians 5:19-21 Speak out to one another in psalms and hymns and spiritual songs, offering praise with voices [and instruments] and making melody with all your heart to the Lord,

At all times and for everything giving thanks in the name of our Lord Jesus Christ to God the Father. Be subject to one another out of reverence for Christ (the Messiah, the Anointed One). AMPC.

Mathew 12:25 And knowing their thoughts, He said to them, Any kingdom that is divided against itself is being brought to desolation and laid waste, and no city or house divided against itself will last or continue to stand. AMPC.

CHAPTER 7
MOVING FORWARD

March 23rd 2012; 29th Adar 5772

Yeshua Speaks: A season of change and innovation is upon you. It seems as though you have stalled in all your pursuits, however for everything there is a time of growth; just as plants need time to reach maturity before bursting forth from the soil to become that which was contained in the seed; so do you.

I have planted and I have watered. I have tended the garden to ensure that when new life bursts forth, it can grow unhindered. Just as there is a perfect time for seeds to be planted so that they will come forth in their right season; so it is in the life of My saints that there is the perfect time when the seed of the Spirit that I have planted will burst forth and blossom in the best conditions for it to reach full maturity.

In seasons of growth there is no point of reference to determine if you are growing or not. In the life of My saints this is called trust and faith; believing that all things will work out and promises will be fulfilled. The ever-expectant hope that this faith will bring the very life and vitality contained within My Word and My promises to you.

The early disciples lived in the expectant hope and assurance that I would come again and each day was filled with an overflowing joy based on My promises to them. The assurance coming from the knowledge that I would never leave them nor forsake them gave them an understanding that the temporary trappings of this life were not a prize to be sought after. They had the joyful assurance that we would be together forever in a world too wonderful for words to explain.

As they came to depend upon Me and Me alone; I showed them little glimpses of the glory laid up for them. Having seen in the spirit and being assured by My Words to them; whatever life brought their way they thought of little consequence in light of the glory and rewards laid up for them.

Many will tell you that you're too old because of your physical age; and your society is cruelly targeting the elderly not valuing them for anything based purely on image and the world's system. There are many who have been hidden for My purposes for the end times. They are unknown to the body of Messiah which in its current form is not yet My true Bride; putting out mixed and confused messages of My true nature. Relationship with Me is developed in the quiet hidden places; the backwaters of life and is dependent upon you coming to know Me, love Me, honour Me, trust Me; no matter what circumstances or what life dictates. Your true value is determined by your relationship with Me and not results.

Life begins anew each and every day. Let your yesterdays be just that. Today and Now, are the only hallmarks and guides that you will need. All your yesterdays with their disappointments, regrets and failures, are just a training ground to bring you to have an absolute trust and faith in Me and Me alone. In what else could you have such assurance? Money in the bank? Investments? Wealth? All these I can give in an instant, but they are not the issue of life. From them only death can proceed if they become the objects of your worship, your desire or your affections. Put your affections on things above not on anything that belongs to this world. I will supply your every need as My Word says and it is surely so. Blessings and favour that you cannot contain are yours. Receive them by faith and cease from your doubting. *Philippians 4:19 Moreover, my God will fill every need of yours according to his glorious wealth, in union with the Messiah Yeshua. CJB.*

It is time to move forward and lay hold of the promises I have spoken. Now is the opening season of your life. Treasures that had been hidden; you will find. Experience the big picture; stop looking at small insignificant situations. I am bigger than all of your problems and trials and sufferings. I am the big picture. It is about Me and what I want to do for you, not what you can do for Me. As much as I appreciate the sentiment of "saved to serve" it is rather insulting to Me that I desire to enslave you rather than as My Word says, "I have come that you may have life and have life to the full!"

John 10:10 The thief comes only in order to steal, kill and destroy; I have come so that they may have life, life in its fullest measure. CJB.

Yahweh Speaks: The problem is not with Me; but in your thinking! When did I ever say you are not worthy? You are worthy because of what I have done and it is insulting to infer that the laying down of My Son's life was not enough to make you worthy of all that I have decided to give you and do for you. You are worthy because I made you worthy. You cannot earn righteousness or right standing with Me by your works. "Simply for the believing" - all of Heaven and its resources are available to you and no other way.

I have done it! Believe it! Receive it! Walk in it! Live it! Stop stumbling along life's highway like a poor blind beggar; tripping up on your own fears and unbelief. Call unbelief what it is – SIN! Confess it and repent of it and start receiving what I have been trying to give you for years. Priceless wine simply for the asking. Simple believing faith is all that is required.

Isaiah 55: 1-11 Wait and listen, everyone who is thirsty! Come to the waters; and he who has no money, come, buy and eat! Yes, come, buy [priceless, spiritual] wine and milk without money and without price [simply for the self-surrender that accepts the blessing].

Why do you spend your money for that which is not bread, and your earnings for what does not satisfy? Hearken diligently to Me, and eat what is good, and let your soul delight itself in fatness [the profuseness of spiritual joy].

Incline your ear [submit and consent to the divine will] and come to Me; hear, and your soul will revive; and I will make an everlasting covenant or league with you, even the sure mercy (kindness, goodwill, and compassion) promised to David.

Behold, I have appointed him (Him) [David, as a representative of the Messiah, or the Messiah Himself] to be a witness [one (One) who shall testify of salvation] to the nations, a prince (Prince) and commander (Commander) to the peoples.

Behold, you [Israel] shall call nations that you know not, and nations that do not know you shall run to you because of the Lord your God, and of the Holy One of Israel, for He has glorified you.

Seek, inquire for, and require the Lord while He may be found [claiming Him by necessity and by right]; call upon Him while He is near.

Let the wicked forsake his way and the unrighteous man his thoughts; and let him return to the Lord, and He will have love, pity, and mercy for him, and to our God, for He will multiply to him His abundant pardon.

For My thoughts are not your thoughts, neither are your ways My ways, says the Lord.

For as the heavens are higher than the earth, so are My ways higher than your ways and My thoughts than your thoughts.

For as the rain and snow come down from the heavens, and return not there again, but water the earth and make it bring forth and sprout, that it may give seed to the sower and bread to the eater, So shall My word be that goes forth out of My mouth: it shall not return to Me void [without producing any effect, useless], but it shall accomplish that which I please and purpose, and it shall prosper in the thing for which I sent it. AMPC.

Yeshua Speaks: Success is a Meaningful Relationship with Me! Results, outcomes, size, wealth, success, popularity are only distractions that people hold up as a meaningful measure of who they are. Many will sit at My side in the Kingdom because they know Me intimately and gave up all to spend more time with Me. Yes there are rewards, but not assessed as is implied by the body of Messiah. Fruit comes because I have planted fruit bearing seed within some of My servants. Who should get the praise, the tree or the Gardener? Who created the seed from which the tree, plant, flower, shrub grew? From whose hands have all your blessings flowed?

Change your focus, put it back to where it belongs, and every day will be a holy day, where I am present with you making each and every moment of everyday a day of companionship and joy overflowing from My heart to yours. Life is for the living. You serve Me best by loving Me and worshipping Me; by acknowledging that all good things have their origins and beginning with Me. I love you and want to pour out upon you liberally, without measure, My great love spilling all over you to draw you to Myself in a never-ending love tryst.

It is time to move forward in My love. Let the past go! It has helped to form you, but it is not who you are. Look into My Word and behold the richness and favour and blessings stored up for all who will love Me and who will let Me love them.

It will require a holy boldness to allow Me to draw near to you and touch you with My love. It will burn you, it will terrify you, it will exhilarate you, and it will change you from the inside out. Come take My hand, don't be afraid anymore. My perfect love for you will cast out every fear. It is time to Move Forward!

CHAPTER 8

DISOBEDIENCE

June 5th 2008; 2nd Sivan 5768.

1 Samuel 15:22-24 Samuel said, Has the Lord as great a delight in burnt offerings and sacrifices as in obeying the voice of the Lord? Behold, to obey is better than sacrifice, and to hearken than the fat of rams.

For rebellion is as the sin of witchcraft, and stubbornness is as idolatry and teraphim (household good luck images). Because you have rejected the word of the Lord, He also has rejected you from being king.

And Saul said to Samuel, I have sinned; for I have transgressed the commandment of the Lord and your words, because I feared the people and obeyed their voice. AMPC.

Yahweh Speaks: To rebel is to disobey Ruach HaKodesh. It is important that you do what Ruach HaKodesh prompts you to do and be obedient to His leading. Not to do so is an act of rebellion and sin. You need to learn to be promptly obedient to Ruach HaKodesh's leadings. No exceptions! No excuses! To obey is better than sacrifice. It is better that you should obey in the first place doing away with the need for a sacrifice to atone for your disobedience. How is it that a child of Mine does not want to come into My presence? Is it because he or she has a wrong understanding of My nature?

I am not a God who punishes, but rather one who loves and forgives first. Yes I will correct you and discipline you, but I always do it with love! Why then do you refuse to meet with Me? You have hurt Me deeply by your rejection. Am I not worthy of your time? What is so important that you cannot meet with Me? Television? The Internet? Movies? Games? The News? I will tell you all that is going on before it happens if you will but spend time with Me. The news you watch will be old news and certainly not worth the time you spend sitting watching it.

There is no greater privilege on this earth than being called into My presence that I may talk with you. From the time spent in My presence you will know what to do in each situation and you will go with My empowering. There is no need to continue to do My work in your own strength as you will fail; and the victory you achieve will only be partial as you did not go in My full authority. You have been doing what you think I want you to do, but it has not been My best for you in the situations you have been in. From this day you must learn to walk in daily obedience if you are to succeed in all My plans for your life.

Begin by praying this prayer of David:

Psalm 51:1-15 For the leader. A psalm of David, when Natan the prophet came to him after his affair with Bat-Sheva:

God, in your grace, have mercy on me; in your great compassion, blot out my crimes.

Wash me completely from my guilt, and cleanse me from my sin.

For I know my crimes, my sin confronts me all the time.

Against you, you only, have I sinned and done what is evil from your perspective; so that you are right in accusing me and justified in passing sentence.

True, I was born guilty, was a sinner from the moment my mother conceived me.

Still, you want truth in the inner person; so make me know wisdom in my inmost heart.

Sprinkle me with hyssop, and I will be clean; wash me, and I will be whiter than snow.

Let me hear the sound of joy and gladness, so that the bones you crushed can rejoice.

Turn away your face from my sins, and blot out all my crimes.

Create in me a clean heart, God; renew in me a resolute spirit.

Don't thrust me away from your presence, don't take your Ruach Kodesh away from me.

Restore my joy in your salvation, and let a willing spirit uphold me.

Then I will teach the wicked your ways, and sinners will return to you. CJB.

Don't let your disobedience separate you from My very best for your life!

CHAPTER 9

I AM THE CATALYST

March 14th 2007; 24th Adar 5767.

Definition: an agent that provokes or speeds significant change or action.

Ruach HaKodesh Speaks: In what is your trust? In your own abilities or Mine?

This is hard to define and many never really learn to trust Me in this lifetime. People give lip service to loving, hearing, and obeying Me; but strong deceptive spirits prevent most from fully entering the joy of the obedient life and the great peace that comes from being in Abba's will.

There is a need for a conscious crossing over; a need to step over the threshold; to enter in; leaving behind all dependence upon self and willing to be guided and led by Me moment by moment, day by day, week in week out, year in year out. When you go your own way; believing that your words or actions in any situation will be the catalyst that makes the difference; you shut off heaven's resources.

I am The Catalyst of Life. I am the One that makes the difference in the hearts and minds of all of mankind. I am limited only by your abandonment to Me and a letting go of all dependence upon self. I will inspire, I will enable, I will teach and I will show you. I will lead you in the way everlasting, full of joy, hope and prosperity; not only for you but for your whole family and all those that come under your authority.

Deuteronomy 28:6 You shall be blessed when you come in, and you shall be blessed when you go out. WEB.

Blessed, blessed, blessed, because I am Abba's blessing to you, upon you, around about you; hedging you in but also freeing you to enjoy freedom of action and divine thinking that you never thought possible. Let Me be the active catalyst in your life that will enrich every minute of your life here on earth, and prepare you for the glorious heavenly experiences that lies ahead.

Mind has not conceived, nor man experienced the fullness of the Godhead, and what is possible both here on earth and in Heaven above. The best that has been recorded is but a foretaste of what can be experienced the moment you enter Heaven. Heaven here and now, it is possible, but you will have to let Me unlock your mind and allow Me to be who I truly am in your life.

You, like many others, limit what I can do for you and through you, because you continually push Me to one side saying; *I will handle this. I feel more comfortable doing it my way*. Well if you keep doing that to Me, just like a good friend, there is a time when I will walk away and that would be sad. Embrace Me, embrace My friendship, love Me and let Me love you. Pull down the barriers that you have raised up. I am not the enemy; I am your best friend. Love Me, talk to Me, and I will answer you, as we walk life's journey together all the way from here to eternity.

I love you but there is a whole new dimension to our relationship that I'm calling you to or rather inviting you to be a part of from this day. Open up your heart; trust Me because I am totally trustworthy. I know you better than you know yourself. I know what makes you tick. I know how you think. I know what makes you you; but further to that I know what Abba wants you to be and do and I am here to help you achieve everything that He has planned for you. It is not over, it is just beginning. You have come through some very trying and difficult times, but all of these events and circumstances are a part of you being guided and led to where you needed to be. You are not alone unless you choose to be alone.

I am available 24/7 night and day, I am right here for you. You don't have to speak to Me, just enjoy My company for this is what our heavenly Abba intended, I am your ever faithful companion. I am your shadow. I will never leave you nor forsake you unless you send Me away. With your invitation I will come back. I don't bear grudges. I am forgiving by nature, but I am very sensitive to your vibes and if I disappear, it is not because I don't want to be around, it will be because I am picking up on what your spirit man is saying. I know when I'm not welcome. Cultivate our friendship from this day; treasure it as I am the greatest treasure that you can have in this lifetime. I will lead you in the way everlasting, full of joy, hope and glory.

The best is yet to come. Don't give up on life but let Me be the active catalyst that makes a difference to every waking moment of life. I am the music of life and you are the song. The two flow together as naturally as sand and surf, fish and water, trees and gardens. You need some new music in your life and that is what I want to be, if you will let Me. Simply by hearing, believing and receiving you will enter into the joy of your Lord. You hold the key in your hand. Unlock your mind and if you don't know how to start or where to begin, give Me the key and I will do the unlocking and all that is necessary to renew your mind.

It begins as an act of faith. You must trust Me with your mind and its workings and I will train you to think differently and break out of the patterns that have you bound which are stopping you from receiving all that Abba wants to give you. I will help you remove the barriers that have stopped you achieving Abba's will. Give Me the key, hand it to Me this day as an act of trust. *Let Me be the Catalyst* that changes the way you think forever for Abba's Glory to be revealed in your life.

John 14:26 But the Counselor, the Ruach HaKodesh, whom the Father will send in my name, will teach you everything; that is, he will remind you of everything I have said to you. CJB.

You can't be rich if you think you don't deserve it. Your mind must be renewed if you are to walk in the style and majesty of your true Abba. A transformation needs to take place so that you can walk, think, act and speak like a King's son or daughter. Let Me begin that work in your life this very day. You are who Yahweh your Abba says you are. Simply believe that you are who Abba says you are and not who others say you are.

These words are the keys for renewing your mind, and you must hear them over and over until they are real to your spirit man. You are who Yahweh your Abba says you are! That is reality. You are not a product of life's experiences or achievements. Positionally you are a son or daughter of Yahweh, a King's Kid, with talents and abilities that come from Yahweh Himself, planted deep within you at the moment of creation.

It's time that they came forth; they are now mature, shaped by life and brought into balance for such a time as this. You will understand these words, in hindsight, but hear, receive, love and obey these words to you, and you will find all that has eluded you, and I am here to help you as your ever faithful companion and active catalyst in your life.

1 Peter 1:23 You have been born again not from some seed that will decay, but from one that cannot decay, through the living Word of God that lasts forever. CJB.

2 Corinthians 5:17 Therefore, if anyone is united with the Messiah, he is a new creation - the old has passed; look, what has come is fresh and new! CJB

Galatians 3:13 The Messiah redeemed us from the curse pronounced in the Torah by becoming cursed on our behalf; for the Tanakh says, "Everyone who hangs from a stake comes under a curse." CJB.

Ephesians 2:10 For we are of God's making, created in union with the Messiah Yeshua for a life of good actions already prepared by God for us to do. CJB

CHAPTER 10

THE BATTLE OF THE MIND

May 24th 2006; 26th Iyyar 5766.

2 Corinthians 10:3-6 For although we do live in the world, we do not wage war in a worldly way; because the weapons we use to wage war are not worldly.

On the contrary, they have God's power for demolishing strongholds.

We demolish arguments and every arrogance that raises itself up against the knowledge of God; we take every thought captive and make it obey the Messiah.

And when you have become completely obedient, then we will be ready to punish every act of disobedience. CJB.

Yahweh Speaks: There are two streams of thought that are continually flowing throughout the earth at any given time. One has its source in Heaven and flows as a river and accompanies Ruach HaKodesh throughout the earth. It is always present and covers the whole earth like a thick cloud. I am present in this cloud and it is My Heavenly network to communicate life, love and light to all of mankind.

My voice is gentle, it is intuitive, it is spontaneous, it is powerful for good and it will set the captives free. It will break asunder the bars of iron, it is inspirational, it is insightful, full of wisdom and knowledge of all things that you need to know in any given instance.

It is the light upon the way, your succourer, and your nurturer. It brings healing and salvation into dark and desperate situations. It leads on to victory and provides a way of escape from the enemy's plans. It will wash you and cleanse you and regenerate not only your mind but your spirit man too. I am all-powerful. I am omnipresent. I am omniscient. The voice of My command is carried gently throughout the earth for those that have trained their ears to hear. *Matthew 11:15 He who has ears to hear, let him hear. WEB.*

You will need to tune and open the ears of your spirit to hear the flow of My voice and behold all that I would show you each and every day of your life. I did not leave you alone as orphans in Satan's kingdom. You are My children and I am speaking to you each and every day but you are not yet clearly hearing My voice. There is another stream of thought that continually bombard your mind day in and day out, night in and night out; until you take authority over this clamour and din you will not be able to hear My voice or have free access to My communication network, My Glory-Net.

My voice network is just like the mountain stream. It is gentle, it is fresh, it is sparkling, and it is continually being renewed from the throne of Heaven itself. Just like accessing a mountain stream you will have to exert effort to climb the mountain to get closer to the pure source of the stream; to enjoy the pristine pleasure of the high places and to get far away from distractions.

As you come up higher and approach the mountain

stream the trees and shrubs that are sparkling with life and nature suddenly become alive; in the higher reaches everything is unspoiled. The rain which comes from above has kissed the earth and the pure white snow caps that are of My design, melt and join with the rains and flow down from the mountain tops to the streams and rivers below. Wherever you are you need to get close to the river and let it touch you.

Learn to shut out the voices that are in your head; challenge them, command them to be quiet. Take authority over the clamour of tongues. Stop agreeing with the thoughts and listen for the gentle spontaneous thoughts that are flowing from My throne room. You will need to spend more time in My word to identify the source of the thoughts. Not all thoughts are evil, just lies mixed with truth. I am truth and My word is true and it stands forever. My truths are eternal. They do not change to suit the occasion or situation. I am not fickle and there is a depth to My words that make them dependable and strong enough to set in place a foundation on which to live.

Tune in to Me by choosing to tune out to Satan. Stop watching and believing the lies and bad reports that are continually portrayed on the media. Satan owns television, the internet, the newspapers and you will not find My voice there or My instructions that you need to fulfil My will for your life. You are told in My word that you must overcome, that you are to be an overcomer and that I am a rewarder of those that do overcome. This is the biggest challenge the body of Messiah Yeshua has to overcome in the last days - The Battle of the Mind.

Romans 12:21 Don't be overcome by evil, but overcome evil with good. WEB.

1 John 5:4 For whatever is born of God overcomes the world. This is the victory that has overcome the world: your faith. WEB.

For too long My people have allowed Satan to run rampant through their minds. He is the master deceiver and he sets out to deceive and enslave the world by cunning and stealth. He has conditioned a whole generation of young people to believe lies, half-truths, and false values and has set in place a foundation of falsehood that will be very difficult if not impossible to eradicate.

But I will overcome and I have overcome; and it is time that My people begin to tune out to Satan; his movies, his internet perversions, his lies propagated on media; and join with Me as we contend with the kingdom of darkness and all that it represents in the world.

Satan's voice is loud and obnoxious. He deliberately turns up the volume wherever My streams are flowing the strongest. As people come to hear My word wherever it is preached, Satan's voice becomes louder. Thoughts such as "I am just wasting my time being here." "God could help me if He wanted to but I know He won't." "I'm not good enough." "No one has experienced what I am going through." "Even God can't help me;" are so loud in people's minds that they cannot hear or receive the words of life, light and love that I speak through My servants.

People need help to turn the voice of Satan down in their lives. You who can, heed the need to help others take authority over Satan's lies and streams of thoughts. Help and instruct them so they can clearly hear My voice for themselves and their loved ones and tune in to Heaven's broadcasts. 2 Corinthians 10:6 instructs you to address your own disobedience first in regard to this most serious of issues. You must begin to do battle in your own mind, over your own house, your own family before you try to help others.

Lead by example, not by principle alone. If you cannot overcome and gain the victory in your own life then you cannot instruct others in what they should do until it is the practice and reality of your own life. Lies will never spawn truth.

Knowing what to do and not doing it is far worse than not knowing what to do at all. You and others have a responsibility to sensitise yourselves to My Ruach HaKodesh. Listen, hear and obey. Watch, look and do only as He leads.

It really is that simple, but the secret is in winning The Battle of the Mind. I have redeemed you and your mind is also redeemed in that act of redemption. Come purify yourselves and purify your minds so that the flow of My thoughts can flow through you and the body of Messiah. Become a part of My Glory-Net. Log on and begin to download My instructions and love communications to you each and every day. It's time to start winning the Battle for your mind!

Getting Started:

Change your thinking habits; ask Ruach HaKodesh to teach you how to think as you should. *Philippians 4:8 Finally, brethren, whatever is true, whatever is honourable, whatever is right, whatever is pure, whatever is lovely, whatever is of good repute, if there is any excellence and if anything worthy of praise, let your mind dwell on these things. NASB.*

Change your friends; don't hang around negative talking friends.

Change your conversation; watch what comes out of your mouth. *Matthew 15:11 What makes a person unclean is* *not what goes into his mouth; rather, what comes out of his mouth, that is what makes him unclean!" CJB.*

James 3:10 Out of the same mouth come blessing and cursing! Brothers, it isn't right for things to be this way. CJB.

Stop thinking from only a human perspective; identify wrong thinking and decide to stop doing it.

Mark 8:33 But, turning around and looking at his talmidim, he rebuked Kefa. "Get behind me, Satan!" he said, "For your thinking is from a human perspective, not from God's perspective!" CJB.

Employ thought police; when bad thoughts are sensed put your thought police to work. Identify the source of your thoughts. Stop agreeing with evil thoughts. Lock the baddies up and throw away the key! Blow the whistle on them!

Excellence; take authority over your thoughts by coming to the light. The Word of Yahweh is a lamp & will expose wrong thinking. Light dispels darkness.

Psalm 119:105 Your word is a lamp to my feet, and a light for my path. WEB.

Pull down strongholds; do not become entangled in the spider's web. Operate only in authority – don't get dragged into arguments or disputes. *1 Timothy 2:8 I desire therefore that the men pray everywhere, lifting up holy hands, without wrath and doubting; NKJV.*

It's time to start winning The Battle Of The Mind!

CHAPTER II

RUACH HAKODESH IS COMING BY TRAIN TOMORROW

November 24th 2009; 7th Kislev 5770.

An Allegory.

How does Ruach HaKodesh come to a city, a person, a community?

Does He arrive unexpectedly and never give an indication as to when He will be coming? No, if your spiritual antennae are working you know He is near, you sense with excitement in your spirit, the inner control panel lights up and joy wells up within you. There is an expectation and anticipation that rises up within you. He is near, you just know it.

If you knew a visitor was coming to your area and you were the one to go and pick them up, you would find out how they are coming. Is it by car, by bus, by plane or by train? You would find out what time they are arriving and make preparations for their visit. But most importantly you would make sure that you were there to greet them when they arrive.

If you know they are coming by plane, you would familiarise yourself with the airport and find out ahead of time where to park, where to pick up the luggage and be prepared. If the person is coming by train, the same principles are put into place to ensure their safe and smooth arrival. You may go to the actual point of arrival and familiarise yourself with all of the practical details well ahead of time, making sure every detail is taken care of.

In the natural you would make sure your car is clean, that it has plenty of fuel and that the boot is empty to accommodate any luggage. You would have checked out the accommodation for your guest and booked it ahead of time, or if they are staying with you prepared the guest bedroom. You would find out what they like to eat and ensure you had their favourite foods available. You would find out about everything that may interest your guest; prepare yourself as best you could before they arrived and as long as they stay you would be prepared to be at their disposal night and day.

Imagine Ruach HaKodesh is coming to stay at your house and He is coming tomorrow and He will be arriving by train. He will be your guest and will stay as long as it pleases Him to do so. What preparations would you need to make to accommodate your invisible guest? He will need free and open access to your computer and the authority to delete any material He may find offensive. This applies to everything in your house. Books, magazines, videos, paintings, decorations, you name it if He doesn't like it, it has to go. Are you up for all of this?

Ruach HaKodesh reads minds and listens to every conversation, so He may have quite a lot to say to you about your thought life as well as idle talk that is contrary in any way to the Holy Scriptures.

Ephesians 4:29 Let no harmful language come from your

mouth, only good words that are helpful in meeting the need, words that will benefit those who hear them. CJB.

Matthew 12:36 Moreover, I tell you this: on the Day of Judgment people will have to give account for every careless word they have spoken; CJB.

2 Timothy 2:16 But keep away from godless babbling, for those who engage in it will only become more ungodly. CJB.

If you displease Him, you may find yourself convicted, even sobbing and weeping uncontrollably and when He communicates with Heaven (which He does constantly) the room may become hazy and you may find yourself prostrate on the floor under a heavy anointing. Angels will be coming and going night and day so I don't know that you will get much sleep.

Ruach HaKodesh loves to worship Yeshua night and day and He may wake you up to join Him. He likes to become totally involved in your life and will go to work with you to meet all your work friends. He will inspire you and enable you to do all things well, and show you ways to introduce others to Yeshua. He is pure genius, pure inspiration and full of zest, so much so that you may find it difficult to keep up with Him. He will show you things from the word you never knew were there. He will teach you how to live life to the full, a life full of joy, hope and endless love. He will show you how to stretch and extend your finances to meet all your needs, and how to sow into the Kingdom of Yahweh that will enrich not only you but countless others.

He will open your eyes to new vistas in Yahweh; He will take you to the rim of Heaven itself so that you can peer into the heavenlies and even see Yeshua and Yahweh in the Throne room of Heaven. He will help you remove the scales from your eyes so that you will be able to look and see and hear and feel the heartbeat of Heaven itself and make plain and open to you all that you have ever desired to know and experience of the coming Kingdom.

He will open the Word to you in a new and intimate way. You will visit often the foot of the execution stake to deal with issues in your own life. There will be sorrow and tears of repentance often as He leads you in the way of holiness, but there will also be joy unspeakable, full of glory as you let Him do His peculiar work in your life. He will help you do Yahweh's will for your life, the good work of faith that is prepared for you. He will be your companion, your catalyst for good, your conscience, your nurturer, your succourer, in fact your everything.

He is coming by train, the Glory Express and He will be here tomorrow and wants to stay at your house. Are you willing and able to go and meet Him and invite Him to come home with you? The train will be arriving shortly after sunrise, at the dawning of your new day in Him.

CHAPTER 12

THE NURSERY GARDEN

May 13th 2025; 15th Iyyar 5785.

An Allegory.

Yahweh's heavenly garden is visited regularly by Himself and His Royal heavenly entourage to savour the ever-changing displays that are coming to maturity.

The garden is beautifully laid out to His divine plan. Every shrub, every boundary tree, every flower and every planting arranged in banks of different colours and different fragrances. The layout of His garden is designed to give all who visit an overwhelming experience not only visually, but also an indescribable powerful aroma of unique fragrances never experienced anywhere, but here in this His garden.

Before the plants are transferred to His royal garden displays, there is a nursery garden nearby, out of sight of the main display area, where the exquisite blooms of budding flowers, plants, and shrubs of all descriptions and origins, are being nurtured, and prepared for their exact placement. Only when they are ready will they be moved to the main display area.

To blossom right on time and right in season requires masterful husbandry and the nursery garden is crucial to preparing, nurturing and feeding the plants the correct nutrients, all the time ensuring the watering is precise and not excessive. Not only the size of the flowers and their peculiar colours is carefully monitored, but also their health ensuring their longevity, whilst on display.

The Nursery Garden: As the plantings are absolutely unique, the seed is harvested from the plants themselves, and they may lay dormant, stored in the nursery's seed bank, until the time of replanting takes place.

Seeds have a central core in which all of the attributes of the flowers or plants are genetically stored. The outer protective layers of the seed will crumble over time effectively dying, but in the process still protect the central core and all its unique properties. The Master Gardener knows each seed intimately and how it needs to be nurtured in its time of dormancy and exactly when it needs to be re-planted.

Many in the body of Yeshua come to a time in their life when there seems to be no way forward as they are. They realise that a major change needs to take place in their lives, but have no idea how this is even possible. But the Master Gardener knows that from death will spring forth new life. In Yahweh's master design the core of the plant or shrub is able to be reborn or re-birthed. The miracle of rebirth and renewal was built into the seed.

John 12:24 "Yes indeed! I tell you that unless a grain of wheat that falls to the ground dies, it stays just a grain; but if it dies, it produces a big harvest." CJB.

And so it is in Yahweh's nursery that which appears to

be dead, can be nurtured, replanted and grow again into the fullness of the Master Designer's blueprint for each season. The new regenerated plant or shrub will grow and be nurtured in Yahweh's nursery to be prepared for the exact time it will be fit to be transferred to the main display. Along with millions of other new and fresh plantings now coming to life, it will be a part of the ever-changing Grand Gardens displays, right on time and right on schedule for Yahweh to enjoy when He comes to visit His gardens.

Regeneration: Can that which appears to be dead come to life? Is there life after death? The garden of Gethsemane witnessed the power of Yahweh setting in place a foundational principle of His Kingdom and the New Covenant. Physical death is not the end, but a transition to and a new beginning in His Kingdom. His Glory has the power over death itself and from physical death eternal life can spring forth. Knowing and believing this truth should turn the fear of death out of doors.

As believers we have the assurance that the fear of death and death itself has no hold over us; it is the birthing into and the beginning of our new eternal life in a new spiritual Kingdom that defies description, explanation or ability to comprehend. Yeshua is the firstborn of His Abba's Kingdom.

1 Corinthians 15:20 But the fact is that the Messiah has been raised from the dead, the firstfruits of those who have died. CJB.

Revelation 1:5 and from Yeshua the Messiah, the faithful witness, the firstborn from the dead and the ruler of the earth's kings. To him, the one who loves us, who has freed us from our sins at the cost of his blood. CJB.

1 Corinthians 15:23 But each in his own order: the Messiah is the firstfruits; then those who belong to the Messiah, at the time of his coming; CJB.

Sometimes we can lose sight of our glorious destiny, trying as it were to just hold on, just existing because we have grown weary of well doing. We feel we are slowly dying, on some kind of a treadmill, struggling from day to day in our daily walk. We need a refreshment, a renewal, but how? We've grown older and tired and can't seem to hear the music of Heaven like we used to.

It's time for our outer protecting layers to be put to death. Just like the seed our outer protection layers that make up what we perceive to be our real selves have to be stripped away.

We need to be planted in Yahweh's nursery garden to be nurtured, watered and supervised by the Master Gardener until our time of breaking forth from the ground, growing into a seedling, into a new, fresh flower or shrub that is ready for replanting in Yahweh's main display gardens for His pleasure and enjoyment.

Dying to self: It's not easy dying to self. On our journey with Yeshua there will be times when it is absolutely essential for us to be ready to die to self; crucifying the outer layers of self so that a new refreshed believer with renewed hope and purpose can burst forth.

The world will look very different when you emerge from the nursery. When you become a part of the new plantings of the Lord, you'll find yourself in the most joyful section of Yahweh's garden.

You will be vibrant because Ruach HaKodesh has visited you and administered the full outworking of Yahweh's salvation plan for you; which has breathed new life into what had become stale.

Your love and appreciation of all the other flowers and shrubs will now bring joy unspeakable to you as your focus will no longer be on just yourself, but for all the other plantings of the Lord.

You'll have a new appreciation of the huge variety and unique beauty of each and every plant. You'll become aware as never before that without the other plantings you are incomplete. You will begin to see and appreciate as Yahweh sees and appreciates each and every plant and the absolute beauty of the combinations of His never-ending creative abilities.

A chorus of praise will sweep across the gardens when He is approaching or when the Master Gardener is in attendance along with thousands of angels and heavenly choirs resplendent in their regalia and the accompanying musical instruments.

You will now sense and see with new eyes and a new awareness of all that has always surrounded you and the context it provided for you, but never been able to appreciate.

It is on the chosen High Holy days when Yahweh and Yeshua, accompanied by myriads of rejoicing angels, that you will know the Master Designer has always had all things in hand.

There will be old and new songs of Heaven, choruses of angels, shofars, harps, heavenly instruments and trumpets sounding fanfares that come with them. They will hold many joyful celebrations in the Master's Gardens that defy human description; a true foretaste of Heaven.

Regenerated and Repurposed: It's time to allow the Master Gardener to replant and regenerate you in His nursery; but you must put to death all that you have relied on up till now and allow Him to nurture and regenerate that which Ruach HaKodesh has imbedded in your DNA.

Allow the process of new growth and new love for

Yeshua and Yahweh to blossom in your life. Submit daily to the leading of Ruach HaKodesh so that you can joyfully fulfil Abba's will for your life.

Move from "Misery Lane to Great Joy Avenue" where the saints are dancing in the streets, preparing their hearts with ever joyful expectation for the soon return of Yeshua the Messiah, the King of Kings, the Lord of Glory, the Prince of Peace, the Son of Righteousness, who comes with healing in His Wings!

Come Yeshua Come!

CHAPTER 13

TURN! TURN! TURN!

October 9th 2011; 11th Tishrei 5772.

Yahweh Speaks: Now is a time of turning for you. Firstly you must turn again and focus on Me. In the busyness of your days you must make time to turn to Me, seek My face, communicate often, but bring the focus off the assignment and back onto Me. As in life there comes a bend in the road and you must turn and follow the road; so in type it is in the realm of the spirit there are bends and turns in the road that you must be careful to follow.

The signpost is before you today telling you to turn. A mission or an assignment comes to an end or the way you have been instructed to do warfare will change, and you must be looking to Me always and often because the battle does change and so do the tactics. You have become dry and thirsty and you need refreshment.

Turn again to My Word and the words that I have spoken to you, they are life, they are truth, they are the light upon your way. Turn again to your family, and enjoy them for your time on earth is so short compared to eternity.

Turn from your fears about the world, your government, your needs and look to Me and Me only in these days. Much confusion will abound at many levels but always ensure that your foundation of faith is rock solid, for I will be the only bastion that will be dependable in these times.

Turn from your worrying and anxiety and be at peace with Me knowing that I have all matters in hand. There is no fear when you know how much I love you and care for you. Perfect love casts out every fear.

1 John 4:18 There is no fear in love; but perfect love casts out fear, because fear has punishment. He who fears is not made perfect in love. WEB.

Have confidence in the words that I have spoken to your spirit, they are truth, they are life, they are health, they are prosperity, they are blessing, they are instructions for your life. Revelations are for you specifically; tailor-made for you because I love you and know who it is that you really are and what you need to make you fulfilled and complete. You are on track. Remember our relationship is not about achievements; it is about My love being made manifest in your life for My Glory and your blessing and enrichment.

Turn from your dependency on your own resources. Ask Me to supply your needs and help you find treasure to share with others and My causes. I have more than enough. Ask in simple believing faith and I will be only too glad and delighted to bless you financially. You have not because you ask not. Living in poverty is no testimony of My enabling power and grace in your life.

Turn from your stubbornness and give in to My promptings. The only person who is suffering is yourself and your family. Why would you want to do that to yourself when so many rich blessings are at your fingertips? I have lavishly provided for you, it's up to you whether you will walk in that or refuse to. I can't make choices for you, that is your department. It is all laid out before you, simply reach out, believe and receive priceless spiritual wine simply for the believing and receiving.

Isaiah 55:1-3 Wait and listen, everyone who is thirsty! Come to the waters; and he who has no money, come, buy and eat! Yes, come, buy [priceless, spiritual] wine and milk without money and without price [simply for the self-surrender that accepts the blessing].

Why do you spend your money for that which is not bread, and your earnings for what does not satisfy? Hearken diligently to Me, and eat what is good, and let your soul delight itself in fatness [the profuseness of spiritual joy].

Incline your ear [submit and consent to the divine will] and come to Me; hear, and your soul will revive; and I will make an everlasting covenant or league with you, even the sure mercy (kindness, goodwill, and compassion) promised to David. AMPC.

Philippians 4:19 Moreover, my God will fill every need of yours according to his glorious wealth, in union with the Messiah Yeshua. CJB.

Yeshua Speaks: There is no catch. Wherever I have planted you remember; this is My city, My state, My nation, My world. On the day of my execution when My precious blood was shed, that entitlement and My authority was passed on to all who will believe. I died so that you can live and redeem the earth and rule wherever your heart desires. It is yours for the asking to enjoy, to bring My presence into your situation wherever you are in the world. All of My servants have been commissioned to redeem and set in place My government over their families, communities, cities and countries. You already have the power to do so, but have not used it.

Change your life, change your home, change your

world, change cities and nations and stop complaining about what Satan is doing. He's only doing what you allow him to do. He has no power to stop you unless you give it to him. He has no authority over you because you are Mine and My blood has redeemed you from the curse and set you on high with Me to rule and reign over this earth and specifically where I have planted you.

Turn from your wrong thinking on this issue and come up higher as I have often invited you to do and enjoy the benefits of My Kingdom and translate it into your world for My Glory and your blessing.

CHAPTER 14

HAS DONE IS DOING WILL DO

February 9th 2011; 5th Adar 1, 5771.

Yeshua Speaks: Being focused on what I have done up till now is indeed a wonderful thing, but precludes the wonderful future hope of glory that you entered into when you began a relationship with Me.

The fullness of our relationship can never be enjoyed until you embrace not only the past and the present, but the promises and fulfilment of all things future, which has not yet fully entered your consciousness. I am the great I Am, encompassing the past present and future.

The future is just as sure as the present, just as the present is as sure as the past. I am at work in the past, today and tomorrow; all the way from eternity past to eternity future and everything in between.

Psalm 41:14 Blessed be Adonai the God of Isra'el from eternity past to eternity future. Amen. Amen. CJB.

Everything pertaining to your life has been planned and provided for before time as you know it began. Tiny intimate details that you have never even recognised as being My provision, have been provided for you ahead of time.

They will materialise in your life as you walk in believing acceptance of My love and provision for you. If you feel abandoned or stranded it is because you have drawn back in unbelief or fear not totally trusting My love and protection and provision for you.

The earth is a stage on which is enacted and played out My relationship with My creation; the work of My hands. It is a transitory place where your relationship with Me is begun. Through suffering you learn to put your trust in Me; as you experience My great love for you, you begin to launch out in love for Me letting go of your former loves and mindsets. Daily you learn to trust Me more with your life, letting go of your own abilities and learning to walk in and trust the supernatural which is My nature. You will learn to distrust your own abilities and look more and more to My abilities.

John 1:3-5 All things came to be through him, and without him nothing made had being.

In him was life, and the life was the light of mankind.

The light shines in the darkness, and the darkness has not suppressed it. CJB.

For a time you must also let go of traditional thinking and allow Me to radically alter your life and as you do you will learn to trust Me as never before. The path for entry into the security that you seek will be found as you completely abandon yourself to Me. What seems to be loss will turn out to be great gain and you will dwell securely in your own place that I will choose for you.

When you look at pictures of the earth from outer space your life seems so insignificant and the passing of your life represents so many turns of the earth. The further you move out through space the smaller the earth and the importance of your life and any relevance or influence you think your life has on the universe fades to almost nothing. But you are a part of the creative force that created the universe. This same massive creative energy is inside of you because you and I are one. You can be as big as the universe or as small as the tiniest atomic particle because I am in all, from the minutest particle of matter to the extent of the whole universe and everything in between. I am all and in all and I am in you.

Let go of your limitations and concentrate on My greatness, My ability, My authority, because it resides in you by faith. You are troubled by your failures and the attacks of the evil one on you and your family. Remember that they treated Me the same way and many that loved Me they falsely accused and put to death. But in Me there is no defeat, no end, only new beginnings. There is no defeat in eternal terms only victory as the powers of darkness and all who resist My divine will and purposes will never prosper or succeed in their evil purposes.

The future has already been written; you are walking out your destiny as planned before time began. Begin to lay hold of this truth and begin to walk in holy boldness and a holy assurance that I have all things in hand. You are not here by chance, it was foreordained.

Psalm 37:23 The steps of a good man are ordered by the Lord: and he delighteth in his way. KJV.

The steps of a good man are ordered by the Lord has a tri-dimensional meaning, incorporating the past, present and future. I do not dwell in time and My Words are not bound by time and should never be limited to the past, or the present. My Words are forever words with power for today and all of your tomorrows in your world all the way throughout My world, My heavens and My coming Kingdom.

You must trust Me and walk by faith if you are to experience Me at a deeper level. More of Me and less of you, allow Me to permeate your being. Let go of the former things and the former way of doing things. Depend upon Ruach HaKodesh as never before.

Ask Me for courage when you are afraid. Ask Me for health and healing for your loved ones. Ask for a home to call your own. Ask Me for life, My life to be released in you each and every day. Ask Me for words of life and for the living water that satisfies. Look to Me, embrace Me, love Me and dare to allow Me to draw near to you and love you with My everlasting love. Just simply enjoy My presence and diligently seek to spend more time with Me and you will find Me.

Jeremiah 29:13 You shall seek me and find me, when you search for me with all your heart. WEB.

Let go of the injustices that are concerning you, because they belong to the past and don't allow them to shape your thinking, or resent what has happened as it will only lead to bondage.

Dwell on My provision for you. You are Mine! The whole earth is Mine and the fullness thereof! *Psalm 50:10 For every animal of the forest is mine and the livestock on a thousand hills. WEB.* But the riches of this world are nothing compared with the treasure of knowing Me. Guard, nurture and embrace this wonderful gift of relationship that you have entered into.

You have not even begun to measure the width, climb the height or plumb the depths of My great love for you. You are Mine and all that is Mine is yours and as you share these riches with others, you will become rich with a wealth that is not of this world. *Matthew 6:19-21 "Do not store up for yourselves treasures on earth, where moth and rust destroy, and where thieves break in and steal. But store up for yourselves treasures in heaven, where neither moth nor rust destroys, and where thieves do not break in or steal; for where your treasure is, there your heart will be also." NASB.*

Store up for yourselves treasures in Heaven, treasure that will last for all eternity, jewels and crowns of My fashioning that will be an adornment for all eternity. Lose your life in Me. Commit your ways afresh to Me this day. Seek Me early, diligently with your whole heart. Come to Me and cry out to Me and I will heal your hurts, and set you free to love Me with total abandon and a freedom you never thought possible.

Remember what I have done for you and in you, but never forget what I am doing in your life, and begin to explore the fullness and the richness of all that I have promised for you in your future, which is My present. I have gone to prepare a place for you, a mansion and an eternal appointment that will blow your mind.

John 14:2 In my Father's house are many places to live. If there weren't, I would have told you; because I am going there to prepare a place for you. CJB.

I am, you are and you will be all that I created you to be, because I have gone before you not only in your world, but Mine and Abba's as well. It has all been planned! Believe it and continue to walk in it by faith day by day. Enjoy, enjoy, enjoy! Live, live, live!

CHAPTER 15
COHANIM

September 16th 2012 after sunset; 1st Tishrei 5773. Rosh Hashanah is here.

Yahweh Speaks: It is the time of setting in place new ideas and new appointments. Many like yourselves have been prepared for such a time as this that is about to befall the world. Those that have no foundation other than that based on fellowship with like-minded believers will fall away in these days. I have appointed My Cohanim to lead My people through this period of history, and I will cause them to be known to those that have dismissed them dishonouring not only their gifting and office, but denigrating them as people, even cutting them off by ridicule and slander.

Remain faithful to the One New Man that I am creating in this hour.

Ephesians 2:14-16 For he is our peace, who made both one, and broke down the middle wall of separation, having abolished in his flesh the hostility, the law of commandments contained in ordinances, that he might create in himself ***one new man*** *of the two, making peace,* *and might reconcile them both in one body to God through the cross, having killed the hostility through it. WEB.*

Stand in the authority of this important office and explore what it means to be chosen as part of My Royal and Holy Priesthood. It is not about position or power in this world; it is about authority in My Kingdom moving at the volition of the King; hearing and receiving instruction from Me and disseminating the word, directions and instructions faithfully to those that have an ear to hear.

Not all will listen as many have become hardhearted, religious and conceited, puffed up with pride and arrogance, because I have used them powerfully in ministry in times past. These are the serpents and vipers that I warned you about in the Scriptures; the poison of their doctrines will lead to death and not life eternal.

Matthew 23:27-33 "Woe to you, scribes and Pharisees, hypocrites! For you are like whitened tombs, which outwardly appear beautiful, but inwardly are full of dead men's bones, and of all uncleanness. Even so you also outwardly appear righteous to men, but inwardly you are full of hypocrisy and iniquity."

"Woe to you, scribes and Pharisees, hypocrites! For you build the tombs of the prophets, and decorate the tombs of the righteous, and say, 'If we had lived in the days of our fathers, we wouldn't have been partakers with them in the blood of the prophets.'

Therefore you testify to yourselves that you are children of those who killed the prophets. Fill up, then, the measure of your fathers. You serpents, you offspring of vipers, how will you escape the judgment of Gehenna?" WEB.

There are subtle half-truths which will lead many astray in these days. Their foundation is head knowledge and not a heart relationship based on life's genuine encounters with Ruach HaKodesh. It will require greater discernment in these uncertain days to ascertain who is genuinely from Me and for Me, because the master deceiver has planted many IEDs *(Improvised Explosive Devices)* in the body of Messiah that are based on false premises and deceptions, varying ever so slightly from the truth, but being delicious deadly delicacies that are full of poison.

Many have had a steady diet of incorrectly interpreted scriptures, based on tradition and even historical events or more precisely their interpretation of how I acted in a certain situation. They have reduced My dealings and outpourings to a method and religious practices that reflect how I dealt with different people at different times in history. They have missed the richness of a relationship with Ruach HaKodesh speaking and moving however He chooses at any particular moment in time. I sent My Son to provide the way where all can freely access Me in plain common language, and enter into realms of maturity and glory where I could reveal Myself in so many different ways, that it would overwhelm them and you all for good.

I delight to enrich you so that you can live life to the full as My Word says. I am come that you may have and enjoy life and have it in abundance. Those are not just comforting words, they are words of life and meaning, revelation and purpose to give you My life. My life in you, a life full of My genius, My provision, My Glory and My healing virtue. A life full of all that I have released for you to enjoy.

How you all have been cheated! Some that touched on it did not freely give it away, but harboured it for themselves to accredit their holiness or their position for gain. These are the ones that will fall in these days, for I am angry that they have deceived, short-changed and fleeced My sheep. Blind guides who once knew the way but took it upon themselves to rule over the hearts and minds of My people;

enslaving and limiting them to their own experiences; excluding the richness and full entitlements that all of My children are meant to enjoy.

John 10:10 The thief comes only to steal and kill and destroy; I came that they may have life, and have it abundantly. NASB-1995.

Never has deception at all levels been so prominent. Wicked men both in the world, and inside the body of Messiah, controlling and deceiving many with wicked lies, half-truths and deception. It is time for My children who are named by My Name to come forth from their places of despair, despondency, disappointment and defeats of the past to begin to shine where I have planted them in these last days.

The plans of evil men prosper when My people remain silent. It is time to enter the fray, come into My presence and get My instructions. It is time to pray as never before and become expert and equipped in the task that I am calling you to.

Don't go out in your own strength or strategies, for you will be cut to pieces. Move only when I tell you to. Train yourself to be accurate and do precisely what I tell you to do. Stay within your boundaries; stay under My wings, stay close, and become strong in Me. It is the hour in which I am appointing My Cohanim.

1 Peter 2:4-5 As you come to him, the living stone, rejected by people but chosen by God and precious to him, you yourselves, as living stones, are being built into a spiritual house to be cohanim set apart for God to offer spiritual sacrifices acceptable to him through Yeshua the Messiah. CJB.

CHAPTER 16
TITHING

January 29th 2007; 10th Sh'vat 5767.

Yahweh Speaks: There is such a thing as pre-emptive tithing, that pre-empts My grace and mercy, which when sown ahead of time by faith, releases the blessings from the storehouse of Heaven.

Tithing in arrears, which is what tithing under the law demands, will ensure My blessings continue. To pre-empt My blessings you will need to sow into the treasury in advance, in expectation of the blessings that are not only financial but spiritual and physical as well. Note that I have instructed you to tithe in advance, because that puts Me under obligation to bless you and I am no man's debtor.

Luke 6:38 "Give, and you will receive gifts — the full measure, compacted, shaken together and overflowing, will be put right in your lap. For the measure with which you measure out will be used to measure back to you!" CJB.

Giving to the poor, sowing into My ministries is like planting seed that will produce fruit for My Kingdom. As you sow into others' lives and ministries, so I will cause others to sow into your life and your ministry. Tithing should be viewed as an action to pre-empt the blessings of Yahweh, taking possession of them by a prepayment of the tithe or the entitlement to blessings. Do you want Yahweh's blessings in arrears or in advance? Stay paid up. Do you want to receive healing before you get sick or after you have experienced illness? Do you want to be rescued from financial difficulties, or do you want to be blessed ahead of time so that you do not get into debt that lessens the blessings of finance.

If tithing is a valid principle of the Kingdom, get it working for you by tithing in advance. How much do you want? Can you outgive Yahweh? Certainly tithe when money comes into your hands and set it aside for the Kings use; but meditate on pre-emptive tithing for My blessings were released to you as a pre-emptive act, to draw you into the Kingdom, so that you could experience My nature first hand. My nature is pre-emptive, I'm looking for someone to bless and I want My nature to rub off on you.

Look for someone to help, a ministry to support, and it will release blessings to you ahead of time and the blessing upon blessings will cause you to increase as you will no longer be My debtor, I will be yours.

Do not come again under bondage to fear, but live in the freedom and life that My Spirit affords. Listen to Ruach HaKodesh and be led by Him and the legal laws will be fulfilled without you having to worry about them. The legalism comes in and curses fall on people because they have been disobedient to the promptings of Ruach HaKodesh, and they thus come out from grace and end up under the law and its penalty.

Tithing is not a tax that I impose on My people. This is a wrong understanding of My nature, but is a view commonly held by many in the body of Messiah. Most do not tithe because they feel I'm taking what rightfully belongs to them; just like another tax to further drain on their hard-earned cash. They have no concept of King and Kingdom and the benefits that I want to pour out on them so they hold on to that which is a product of their own hands, and the fruit of their labour, and thus limit the blessings to just money. Health, prosperity of spirit, the ability to help others, spiritual gifts, talents and abilities have little or no meaning to them and tithing is regarded as an imposition by an uncaring God.

Money is really not the issue; it is the understanding of My nature; which is one of generosity and life and health and peace and great blessings. With whatever you give back to Me, I multiply it and return it to you, over and over. I sanctify it, bless it, multiply it and return it to you, with blessings.

It is seed that if given in a correct attitude I can use to bless not only you, but all who are in the Kingdom. It's not the amount of money that matters, it is the attitude it is given with, for I love a cheerful giver, because that is who I am. I am cheerful. I am joyful. I am generous and I want you to be too. Don't short change Me, for in so doing, you will only short change yourself.

Tithing is an attitude of the heart, not a percentage of your income!

2 Corinthians 9:7 Let each man give according as he has determined in his heart, not grudgingly or under compulsion, for God loves a cheerful giver. WEB.

CHAPTER 17

THE RISING

Easter Sunday March 30th 2013; 19th Nissan 5773. Pesach day four. You have entered the time known as The Rising.

1 Corinthians 15:54-58 When what decays puts on imperishability and what is mortal puts on immortality, then this passage in the Tanakh will be fulfilled:

"Death is swallowed up in victory.

"Death, where is your victory?

Death, where is your sting?"

The sting of death is sin; and sin draws its power from the Torah; but thanks be to God, who gives us the victory through our Lord Yeshua the Messiah!

So, my dear brothers, stand firm and immovable, always doing the Lord's work as vigorously as you can, knowing that united with the Lord your efforts are not in vain. CJB.

Yeshua Speaks: The adversary is rising in the world progressing his plans to kill and destroy the works of My hands and all of mankind. He hates the liberated ones who look only to Me for their daily sustenance, and is determined to interfere with My plans for good. Although he is rising, I too am rising, and I am calling for all of My chosen ones to come and rise up with Me and rise above the circumstances and events that are even now befalling the earth. Yes there is weather manipulation, there is corruption such as the world has never seen, there is a planned destruction and annihilation of all of the works of My hands and My people. But as wicked and powerful as Satan is, he is no match for the King of Glory and My glorious ones in these last days.

Never forget that My army of angels and the Hosts of Heaven can intervene and turn impossible situations around in the twinkling of an eye. When you stand on the wall in these last days as My watchman, keep your eyes on the King, not the evil workings of the wicked one. He has no power other than that which I allow. There are lines he cannot cross over. He is not all-powerful. His days are numbered as scripture plainly states and these days of his tyranny and rebellion will be terrible but short; for the culmination of the scriptures and history is happening all around you.

Revelation 20:2-3 And he laid hold of the dragon, the serpent of old, who is the devil and Satan, and bound him for a thousand years; and he threw him into the abyss, and shut it and sealed it over him, so that he would not deceive the nations any longer, until the thousand years were completed; after these things he must be released for a short time. NASB-1995.

Revelation 12:12 "For this reason, rejoice, O heavens and you who dwell in them. Woe to the earth and the sea, because the devil has come down to you, having great wrath, knowing that he has only a short time." NASB-1995.

The wickedness that has remained hidden is now

blatantly being displayed as some kind of badge of honour. Hidden things are being revealed and many people's hearts are attracted to the boldness of leadership sold out to paedophilia, homosexuality, population reduction, murder, wars, debaucheries of all kinds because in their heart of hearts there was always the seeds and roots of evil seeking expression.

Now, in this time, all the hidden things are being magnified and many evil manifestations are and will continue to come out in the open. More and more people are coming out, revealing hidden perversions, abominations and wickedness that they have been practicing in secret for many years. They desire to flaunt their filthiness for all to see, believing that their very corruptness will promote them in the eyes of their peers, scorning all who would label them as perverted, declaring themselves to be liberated or enlightened. They are in positions of power and have already changed the laws of their countries to accommodate and promote their vile practices and wicked agendas.

Luke 8:17 For nothing is hidden that will not become evident, nor anything secret that will not be known and come to light. NASB.

Romans 1:29-32 being filled with all unrighteousness, wickedness, greed, evil; full of envy, murder, strife, deceit, malice; they are gossips, slanderers, haters of God, insolent, arrogant, boastful, inventors of evil, disobedient to parents, without understanding, untrustworthy, unloving, unmerciful;

and although they know the ordinance of God, that those who practice such things are worthy of death, they not only do the same, but also give hearty approval to those who practice them. NASB-1995.

This will increase until the cup of the abominations is

full and the evil one is fully revealed along with all of his evil and wicked plans for the destruction of all humankind. He will continue until the day of Armageddon and you cannot comprehend his wickedness that is only beginning now to be revealed. It must be open and plain for all to see who he is and what he intends to do with the earth and all of mankind. In this revealing many will see plainly the choice of My great love or his tyranny. The choice between real life, My life, life eternal or his life, a transitory journey that leads only to disappointment, disillusionment, despair and death - eternal death.

In this time of troubling many will be saved, it is not all doom and gloom. All the things being stripped away are but the temporary trappings of life. To enable you to continue to serve Me, I will provide, I will guide and I will direct you through these uncertain times.

Keep your eyes on the King, seek to obey His commands. Remember always to live in the victory that was won for you on the execution stake. Victory is a state of mind, knowing that you have the legal entitlement to all of the resources of the King, to be used at His discretion. Don't be intimidated by lack and want or his evil threats in these last days. Yes you are to be as wise as serpents and as gentle as doves, and you will be as long as you stay close to Me and take your eyes off the adversary.

1 Corinthians 15:57-58 but thanks be to God, who gives us the victory through our Lord Yeshua the Messiah!

So, my dear brothers, stand firm and immovable, always doing the Lord's work as vigorously as you can, knowing that united with the Lord your efforts are not in vain. CJB.

Matthew 10:16 "Behold, I send you out as sheep in the midst of wolves; so be shrewd as serpents and innocent as doves." NASB-1995.

This is the time of My rising in the world. I desire for all My children also to rise with Me in these days. This Easter Sunday as you practice it, is the day that you celebrate My rising or My resurrection. You call it Resurrection Sunday. But My life did not end with My body departing the earth. I rose so that you too can rise. I am the Firstborn and I have gone ahead of you to prepare a place and position for you here in the Kingdom of Heaven.

John 14:2-3 In My Father's house are many dwelling places; if it were not so, I would have told you; for I go to prepare a place for you. If I go and prepare a place for you, I will come again and receive you to Myself, that where I am, there you may be also. NASB-1995.

I have an appointment lined up for each and every one who believes. I am eternal, you also are eternal but you must rise up from your deadness and begin to put off the grave clothes that Satan is trying to dress you in.

1 Peter 1:3-4 Praised be God, Father of our Lord Yeshua the Messiah, who, in keeping with his great mercy, has caused us, through the resurrection of Yeshua the Messiah from the dead, to be born again to a living hope, to an inheritance that cannot decay, spoil or fade, kept safe for you in heaven. CJB.

Put off despair, despondency, desperation, disappointment, disillusionment, death, defeat and destruction. They are not from Me. Do you see these things in My Word? When was I ever defeated? Was the execution stake a defeat or the greatest victory? Rejoice then in your execution stake for it will lead you onto your greatest victory. If you embrace it, it will allow you to rise up above your circumstances and break the grip and limitations that life here on earth has on you. It will allow you to live with Me in the heavenly places. *Matthew 10:38 And anyone who does not take up his execution-stake and follow me is not worthy of me. CJB.*

Focus on the victory. I am the victorious one. Live in the victory of My resurrection. The same power that raised My lifeless human body back to life is available for you and your loved ones. But that rising from physical death is not the full picture. I was translated and went to live in the presence of My Abba to daily fellowship with Him, to sit in His presence face-to-face and enjoy all the benefits of His Kingdom. This is a greater revelation of My resurrection that I want you to grasp this Resurrection Sunday.

Romans 8:11 And if the Spirit of the One who raised Yeshua from the dead is living in you, then the One who raised the Messiah Yeshua from the dead will also give life to your mortal bodies through his Spirit living in you. CJB.

Mark 16:19 So then the Lord, after he had spoken to them, was received up into heaven and sat down at the right hand of God. WEB.

Look beyond this life; look to the promises of restored fellowship with the Creator of the universe; the creator of you. Remember that you were created by Him, for Him and His enjoyment. All of your achievements here on this earth whether social, financial or even that which has been achieved for Him will fall away the moment that you behold Him face-to-face. Your struggles, your pain, your troubles, your disappointments, the despairing simply melt away when you understand that the purpose of this life is so that you can die to all of these things and simply have one ambition, to be in His presence or near Him every moment of every day, forever!

The rising must occur in your heart of hearts, in the deepest innermost chambers of your true self, that you spend so much time and effort trying to make acceptable to Him. Come rise with Me this day, but not to the limitations of a better life, or a more dedicated life, or a more religious life or even a more serving life. Come rise with Me past the limitations of this life and its concerns and focus on the world to come.

Focus more on the coming Kingdom, seek the face of Abba. Experience His wonderful gift of eternal life, the essence of Heaven itself. Come into My presence and I will show you My Abba. He is releasing His heavenly nature, power and resources as never before to enable you to cope with the short time that you have left on this earth and the tribulations that are even now befalling a fallen world. Heaven is full of the Glory of My Abba, and you must rise and experience Heaven itself and begin speaking and bringing the Glory of the Kingdom into your daily situations.

Defeat, Darkness, Disillusionment, Despair, Despondency, Danger, Death and Destruction all begin with the letter 'D' and are the attributes of the devil. There is no devil in Heaven and all of these 'D' words are never spoken up here. You need to de-devil your life and speech. Get rid of the devil's "Ds".

Begin today to renew your thinking and your speaking;

- Focus on the Fantastic
- Focus on the Fabulous
- Focus on the Favour
- Focus on the Fragrances of Heaven
- Focus on the Future and appropriate its benefits by faith now

I am not bound by time and as you come to know Me you can sneak into your future and take some of the favour and fortunes and take them back to your life. "Back to the future" - so to speak, remembering that I and My Abba are your future and you can begin living in your future taking as it were, privileges and provisions that are stored up for you. Where do you think healing, deliverance, miracles, faith and favour come from anyway? Someone simply stepped into the future and took a little bit of Heaven and released it by faith into their current situation.

Ephesians 2:10 For we are of God's making, created in union with the Messiah Yeshua for a life of good actions already prepared by God for us to do. CJB.

"Think outside of the square" is an earthly expression that indeed has heavenly realities. If your journey involves suffering, you will receive the grace and mercy to endure the path that Abba has laid out for you to walk. My obedience to Abba was perfected by suffering and as intense as it was, it lasted but a short time in the light of eternity. My Word should not be interpreted as meaning you will have a life free of pain and suffering, which often permeates most saints' journeys in life; they are to point you to the wonderful hope and assurance of Abba's ever present enabling Ruach HaKodesh. He is your companion, counsellor and constant contact releasing all of the resources of Heaven for all that Abba has called you to do.

Simply believe and you will receive. Daily develop your relationship with Ruach HaKodesh and allow Him to guide you into Abba's perfect will for you and yours. There are many watchmen on the walls in these last days telling you of all the evil that is becoming more and more evident across the globe. But be careful to seek My counsel in all matters in these days. Yes the enemy is rising in the world, plainly for all to see, but I am rising too, and I will not leave you abandoned in these perilous times.

Joshua 1:5 No man shall be able to stand before you all the days of your life; as I was with Moses, so I will be with you. I will not leave you nor forsake you. NKJV.

Matthew 21:22 And all things you ask in prayer, believing, you will receive. NASB-1955.

Remember that it is right and appropriate for watchmen to be on the wall to warn of the approaching enemy, but remember that Elisha was not on the wall, he was in My presence. It was a man of Yahweh that the king sought in the time of danger.

"What is the Counsel of the Lord?"

"What am I to do in this situation?"

Keep your eyes on the King. Seek to be in His presence. No matter how threatening the evil one may seem to be, do not be drawn into any plans or actions of your own based in fear; because the enemy will have you right where he wants you, trapped in his kingdom of fear.

Romans 8:15 For you didn't receive the spirit of bondage again to fear, but you received the Spirit of adoption, by whom we cry, "Abba! Father!" WEB. {footnote: Abba is an Aramaic word for "Father" or "Daddy", which can be used affectionately and respectfully in prayer to our Father in heaven.}

- The only antidote for fear is faith.
- Faith in the Faithful One
- Faith in His counsel
- Faith in His Ruach HaKodesh
- Faith in His Son
- Faith in His Word
- Faith in His Great Kingdom
- Faith in His power
- Faith in His provision
- Faith in His protection
- Faith in His healing

- Faith in His strength
- Faith at all levels in Yahweh El-Shaddai

Develop your faith in these days of the rising of the evil one, and focus on My rising. Rise with Me in these days and enjoy the resurrection power that overcomes and leads onto My glorious victory. Let Me rise in your heart. Let My Ruach HaKodesh indwell and permeate you; percolating as it were in your spirit; alive and active inspiring and counselling you in these uncertain days.

2 Timothy 1:7 For God did not give us a spirit of timidity (of cowardice, of craven and cringing and fawning fear), but [He has given us a spirit] of power and of love and of calm and well-balanced mind and discipline and self-control. AMPC.

When you're on the wall as a watchman, bring your news into the presence of Ruach HaKodesh and seek His counsel. Never be overwhelmed by what you are seeing and always remember the story of Elisha's servant who panicked when he saw the enemy surrounding them. Elisha prayed that Yahweh would open the servants eyes so that he could see the fiery army of angels surrounding and greatly outnumbering the enemy. Never forget the truth of this story, never doubt the reality of Abba's Kingdom and His power at any time to provide for and protect all that concerns you.

2 Kings 6:15-17 And when the servant of the man of God arose early and went out, there was an army, surrounding the city with horses and chariots. And his servant said to him, "Alas, my master! What shall we do?"

So he answered, "Do not fear, for those who are with us are more than those who are with them." And Elisha prayed, and said, "Lord, I pray, open his eyes that he may see." Then the Lord opened the eyes of the young man, and he saw. And behold, the mountain was full of horses and chariots of fire all around Elisha. NKJV.

Be faithful to fulfil your commission and calling. Do not be concerned about the enemy, but focus on pleasing the King and completing your work here on earth; for the night is coming when your work will be done and you will all step over into the place that is even now being prepared for you. Don't focus too much on the hows and whys, but focus on being obedient to the leading of Ruach HaKodesh as never before in these most uncertain times.

John 9:4 We must work the works of Him Who sent Me and be busy with His business while it is daylight; night is coming on, when no man can work. AMPC.

Always remember what I told My disciples that I was sending them Ruach HaKodesh. *John 16:7-15 But I tell you the truth, it is to your advantage that I go away; for if I do not go away, the Helper will not come to you; but if I go, I will send Him to you. And He, when He comes, will convict the world concerning sin and righteousness and judgment; concerning sin, because they do not believe in Me; and concerning righteousness, because I go to the Father and you no longer see Me; and concerning judgment, because the ruler of this world has been judged.*

I have many more things to say to you, but you cannot bear them now. But when He, the Spirit of truth, comes, He will guide you into all the truth; for He will not speak on His own initiative, but whatever He hears, He will speak; and He will disclose to you what is to come. He will glorify Me, for He will take of Mine and will disclose it to you. All things that the Father has are Mine; therefore I said that He takes of Mine and will disclose it to you. NASB-1995.

I have not left you alone in this world as orphans or without a guide. Embrace Ruach HaKodesh as never before.

He will be your only anchor in the days that lie ahead. Be promptly obedient to His leadings. Train your spirit to be in tune with Him.

John 16:33 "I have said these things to you so that, united with me, you may have shalom. In the world, you have tsuris. But be brave! I have conquered the world!" CJB.

It is the season of The Rising.

CHAPTER 18

HEAVEN IS LEAKING

February 26th 2014; 26th Adar 1, 5774.

Ruach HaKodesh Speaks: Heaven is leaking the Glory and manifest presence of El Shaddai. Heaven is bursting at the seams, barely able to contain the Glory that is intensifying as all is made ready for Heaven's armies to be released on the command of Abba. All is in readiness for the King of Kings to mount up and lead Heaven's angelic hosts to their strategic positions before the great end time battle of Armageddon.

Backing up the armies of Heaven are hosts of caravans loaded with supplies to occupy the earth after the battle. The battle signals the beginning of the millennial reign of the Messiah and hosts of angels are even now being given their assignments over provinces and nations to rule them in righteousness, justice and truth. Messiah Ben Joseph has become Messiah Ben David. This time He will come in the fullness of the power of the Kingdom as the conquering King establishing His Kingdom by the fire and glorious power present at the creation of all things.

Satan, that dog, will be defeated by Him who comes in

His great power and who will defeat all the armies of the world gathered against Him. Satan will be defeated and his illicit reign as king of the earth will end in an instant, in a flash, as Holy fire from the mouth of Yeshua HaMashiach will consume the armies of the earth. The battle will be short and decisive and the focus will move quickly onto establishing and resourcing King Yeshua's new Kingdom and His thousand-year reign.

Revelation 20:1-3 Next I saw an angel coming down from heaven, who had the key to the Abyss and a great chain in his hand.

He seized the dragon, that ancient serpent, who is the Devil and Satan [the Adversary], and chained him up for a thousand years.

He threw him into the Abyss, locked it and sealed it over him; so that he could not deceive the nations any more until the thousand years were over. After that, he has to be set free for a little while. CJB.

Come Yeshua, Come!

EPILOGUE

The Aaronic Blessing:
Numbers 6:24-26 CJB.

'Y'varekh'kha Adonai v'yishmerekha.

May *Adonai* bless you and keep you.

Ya'er Adonai panav eleikha vichunekka.

May *Adonai* make his face shine on you and show you his favor.

Yissa Adonai panav eleikha v'yasem l'kha shalom.

May *Adonai* lift up his face toward you and give you peace.

AFTERWORD

2 Corinthians 10: 3-5 For although we do live in the world, we do not wage war in a worldly way; because the weapons we use to wage war are not worldly.

On the contrary, they have God's power for demolishing strongholds. We demolish arguments and every arrogance that raises itself up against the knowledge of God; we take every thought captive and make it obey the Messiah. CJB.

It is time you begin to take responsibility for your thought life. The complete plan of salvation includes the renewing of your minds and gives every believer access to all of Heaven's resources. The only reason they are not flowing in your life is that you remain bound by earthly thinking, or thinking below the line. Although born again, the life you are now living can fall far short of the fullness of what Yahweh has planned and provided for all who will continue to grow in faith and be willing to be led by Ruach HaKodesh.

Don't continue to blame others or life's circumstances to excuse you from growing into the person that God intended you to be. The gifts that lie dormant within your spirit will not grow unless they are watered with the Word and nurtured with the desire to walk in the fullness that God intended. It is up to you to do all that you can to discover and grow into the real you. A complete abandonment of selfish, soulish goals will set you on this journey.

Above the Line Thinking will begin for you when you take responsibility for your own actions and shortcomings; admit that you cannot be the real you that God created you to be until you allow Ruach HaKodesh to take control of your thought life. If you are willing He will lead and school you in the way everlasting and help you to grow each day in your love of Yeshua to become more like Him. You must make the choice and make yourself available. Don't let your unbelief, or Satan's lie that all the gifts of the Ruach HaKodesh, miracles, healings, provision, protection outlined in the Word are not for you or are out of your reach.

As you begin to think above the line and align your thoughts with the thoughts of Heaven, you will be delighted as all the unexplored resources of Ruach HaKodesh begin to manifest themselves in your life.

It is time to look up, think up, act up, believe up, worship up, praise up Above the Line of your current thinking. Lay hold of all that Abba has built into your spirit the very day that He created you. His plans for your life and all the resources that you will need to fulfil His will for your life were made available to you the very day you invited and received His Son Yeshua into your heart and life.

The thoughts of Heaven and the resources of Heaven will be released to your spirit when they are needed.

The operation of the gifts of Ruach HaKodesh and divine revelation from the Word, provision and protection will grow and be established in your life as you abandon yourself to the leading of Ruach HaKodesh and allow your thoughts to align with His.

1 Cor 12:7-11 "Moreover, to each person is given the particular manifestation of the Spirit that will be for the common good.

To one, through the Spirit, is given a word of wisdom; to another, a word of knowledge, in accordance with the same Spirit;

to another, faith, by the same Spirit; and to another, gifts of healing, by the one Spirit;

to another, the working of miracles; to another, prophecy; to another, the ability to judge between spirits; to another, the ability to speak in different kinds of tongues; and to yet another, the ability to interpret tongues.

One and the same Spirit is at work in all these things, distributing to each person as he chooses." CJB.

Abba wants you to fulfil all that he has equipped you with so that, just like His Son Yeshua, you too will complete His perfect will for your life. He will enable you to do that which is impossible in the natural; so that His Glory will be demonstrated to all who come into contact with you, His sons and daughters. The hour is late and so it is urgent that you all begin to think above the line of natural thinking to be supernaturally enabled to do Abba's will. Let go of the past; stop looking around and being bound by day-to-day opposition to the real you Yahweh is shaping.

Come up higher and begin to develop a heavenly perspective on your life, your future and Abba's will for your life. Season your prayers with heavenly wisdom and direct them at the powers of darkness, and not at people.

Untangle yourself from your own problems and others' problems looking past day-to-day events and always to the future. Direct your prayers to what will be, and not what has been, or is currently happening in your life and the world.

See as Abba sees. Decree and live in the victory won at Calvary over the unrighteous acts of others, and the circumstances of life. Remember that Satan has already been defeated, so change your thinking and begin living a victorious overcoming life; free your mindset from bondage to past events and regrets.

Ask Ruach HaKodesh to renew your mind daily and launch out in faith to begin a new revitalised outlook on life from Heaven above through the eyes of Abba who dwells outside of time.

Learn to align your thinking with the thoughts of Heaven; rejoice and live in the victory that has already been won for you by Yeshua.

Let go of your current thinking patterns; challenge them, and cause them to line up with the thoughts of Heaven. Align your mind's thinking and your thoughts with the mind of the Messiah and His way of thinking.

It is time to begin your journey of retraining your mind to think above the line as you allow Ruach HaKodesh to be the catalyst that will change the way that you think forever for Abba's Glory to be revealed in your life.

Thomas A Petterson

Prophetic Scribe

ABOUT THE AUTHOR

Thomas Petterson comes from a family with a rich Christian heritage. His Great Grandfather, Colonel Sharpe, was known as the Fiery Prophet in the Salvation Army. Thomas was raised in the Salvation Army; at age seven his family moved to the Pymble Baptist Church where he spent most of his teenage years.

At age sixteen he was drawn to the bedside of his recently departed grandmother, knelt down and gave his life to Jesus. Many years later he discovered that his grandmother had been praying for her grandsons to be saved and filled with the Holy Spirit.

Thomas spent the next decade searching for a deeper relationship with God. He was baptised in the Holy Spirit at a Holy Spirit Teaching Seminar in Sydney in 1976 where his life took on a whole new dimension. He married his sweetheart Julie-Ann in 1977 and joined by God as a team; they have been following Him wherever He has directed them.

In 1981 he left the family business and Thomas began the journey of discovering who he was in Jesus Christ. Together, with his wife Julie-Ann, they bought a motel in Nowra; it was in the office of the complex one morning as he was meditating, praying and looking at the Nowra bridge across the river he started to write down what he heard the Holy Spirit say....... "Just as the bridge you are looking at is 100 years old"....Thomas thought that's ridiculous, screwed up the paper and threw it in the bin.

The next day the local paper ran a front-page article on how the bridge was 100 years old and had been re-opened after renovations. He realised that he really had heard from the Lord and needed to start taking notice of what the Holy Spirit was telling him.

G.I.F.T Godly Insights For Today is a result of over 40 years of listening to the Holy Spirit.

During the late 60s & 70s, Thomas was the technical director for Young World Singers who conducted evangelistic outreach concerts across Australia, New Zealand, South East Asia and Papua New Guinea.

He attended Vision Christian College and holds a Certificate in Biblical Studies with honours 1998; Associate Diploma in Biblical Studies with Honours 1998; Diploma in Ministry with honours 1999 and Diploma in Theology with Honours 2001.

Together with his wife ran a Christian Convention Centre in Nowra and established and ran a Christian Parent Controlled School on the NSW South Coast.

They became qualified prayer counsellors through VMTC Victorious Ministries Through Christ in 1986 and volunteered as counsellors for 5 years. Music has been a big part of their lives, running music groups, children's choirs, concerts, Christian art exhibitions and prayer fellowships.

A family trip to Israel in 1989 added another dimension to his spiritual life and sent him on a fresh journey to discover the Hebrew roots of his Christian faith.

Thomas has been married to Julie-Ann for over 45 years and they now reside in Canberra, Australia.

ALSO BY THOMAS A PETTERSON

G.I.F.T. eBook Seasons 1-8

https://giftbook.net/buy-now/

G.I.F.T. Season Nine: Troubled Waters Dead Ahead

The world is now entering Troubled Waters as the master of evil is inspiring his legions of fallen angels to commit unthinkable atrocities around the globe.

Don't let attacks, whether they be physical, emotional or spiritual, deter you from becoming the real you, united with Abba through Yeshua, led and directed by Ruach HaKodesh each and every day, every step of the way, led and fed supernaturally through these trying and testing times.

G.I.F.T. Season Eight: The Shaking & Awakening

The shofars are sounding! Let all who have ears to hear; heed the sound of the heavenly shofars calling all God's people everywhere; to prepare for what is soon to befall the world.

The body of Messiah has become complacent and needs to heed the ancient warning of the Jewish sages to wake up from our slumber and realise that the enemy has infiltrated the camp. There are many walking wounded some injured by friendly fire! Whatever happened to our understanding that we are at war with the dark kingdom?

www.ingramcontent.com/pod-product-compliance
Lightning Source LLC
LaVergne TN
LVHW051010080826
845145LV00009B/2560

* 9 7 8 1 7 6 4 2 4 4 9 3 0 *